The Apostles' Creed

BOOKS BY WOLFHART PANNENBERG
Published by The Westminster Press

The Apostles' Creed:
  In the Light of Today's Questions

Theology and the Kingdom of God

Jesus—God and Man

*In collaboration
  with Avery Dulles and Carl E. Braaten*

Spirit, Faith, and Church

Wolfhart Pannenberg

The Apostles' Creed

In the Light of Today's Questions

THE WESTMINSTER PRESS
Philadelphia

Translated by Margaret Kohl from the German

© SCM Press Ltd 1972

Second printing, 1975

Published by The Westminster Press®
Philadelphia, Pennsylvania

Printed in the United States of America

Library of Congress Cataloging in Publication Data

Pannenberg, Wolfhart, 1928–
    The Apostles' Creed: in the light of today's questions.

    Translation of Das Glaubensbekenntnis, ausgelegt
und verantwortet vor den Fragen der Gegenwart.
    1. Apostles' Creed. I. Title.
BT993.2.P3513   238'.11   72-5767
                                    ISBN 0-664-20947-5

Contents

Foreword

This interpretation of the Apostles' Creed, which I am here laying before a wider circle, was originally a series of lectures for members of all faculties, which I gave several times from 1965 onwards. The purpose of this interpretation is to offer suggestions for forming a contemporary judgment about the content of the credal formulae which many Christians still repeat Sunday by Sunday in church. If this is to be possible, three things are needed: in the first place, the basic factual information about the original meaning of the formulations; secondly, clues as to how the articles of faith mentioned in the creed can be regarded in the light of today's critical biblical scholarship; and thirdly, a consideration of the possible meaning of the substance of the creed for the Christian today in the context of the problems and convictions of the present under-standing of reality.

The text of the Apostles' Creed, whose sections head the separate chapters, is based on the German version in the Luth-eran confessional writings, and is still in use in the Lutheran churches today. Because it does better justice to the sense of the original Latin text, however, I have talked in the third article about the communion (not community) of saints and about 'a holy catholic (or universal) church', whereas the 'Reformed' substitution of 'Christian' for 'universal' is only taken account of in parentheses. In the age of the ecumenical movement, the general character of the church must no longer count as an attribute belonging to one section of the church alone; it must once more be understood as basic to the church as a whole, especially since it provides the foundation for the expansion of the Christian church beyond its own barriers to the whole of mankind. In the case of the projected ecumenical joint version of the German Apostles' Creed, I should also have had to make alterations – or one alteration at least – for factual reasons: the ancient formula 'descended into hell' says something more and something deeper than 'descended into the realm of the dead'.

The expert reader will notice that I have modified my views at certain points. I should like expressly to draw attention to one alteration, which goes deeper than the others. In my book *Jesus – God and Man*, I represented the rejection of Jesus by the Jewish leaders of his day as being the result of his criticism of the Law; and I went on to remark that the raising of Jesus, therefore, conversely put the Law in the wrong and to that extent meant (in principle) the end of the Jewish religion. Today I regret this conclusion, which seemed to me inescapable at the time. It involved the presupposition of a view widespread in German Protestantism, that the religion of the Law and the Jewish religion are identical. I have meanwhile learnt to distinguish between the two. I think that I can see how for the Jewish faith, too, the God of Jewish history can stand above the Law. For it is only in this way that the earthly activity of Jesus can be also understood as a Jewish phenomenon. It is obvious that this recognition makes possible greater open-mindedness towards dialogue between Christians and Jews, since it takes account of the broad common basis which spans the Christian-Jewish contrasts.

To all those who have encouraged me to revise and print these lectures for a wider public I should like to express my thanks; and especially to my wife.

Munich, January 1972

I Believe

When in the early church, from the second century onwards, a man said 'I believe', using the words of what we today know as the Apostles' Creed (or one of its earlier forms), he had as a rule the preparatory instruction for baptism behind him. Three questions were put to the second-century candidate for baptism: 'Do you believe in God, the Father Almighty? Do you believe in Jesus Christ, our Saviour? Do you believe in the Holy Spirit, a holy church, and the forgiveness of sins?' If he answered these questions with a threefold 'I believe', he was baptized, on this confession of faith, in the name of the triune God to whom the three parts of the creed relate.

The earliest form of our creed was the baptismal affirmation of faith of the church in Rome. At first it took the form of question and answer. From the third century onwards it was spoken as a continuous text by the baptismal candidate. In the early period of the church this was by no means the only baptismal creed of its kind. A whole number of similar credal formularies are known, each of which must be regarded as being the baptismal affirmation of faith of some particular local church. Formularies of this kind have come down to us from as early as the second century. Certain fragments, quoted in the New Testament writings, have even been preserved from the first century. The Rome creed – and still more its final form in today's Apostles' Creed – is therefore by no means the oldest of all Christian formularies; it is not apostolic, in the sense that it was formulated word for word by Jesus' disciples. But it claims to be apostolic in another sense, namely as being the appropriate summing up of the message passed down by the apostles. With this claim the baptismal creed of the church in Rome has found widespread acceptance, at least in the sphere of Western Christ- endom. Charlemagne prescribed an expanded version of the text for use in church services throughout the whole Carolingian empire, and in the ninth century this form of the text was taken over by Rome as well. The Reformers accepted the Apostles' Creed as the basis of their faith also, and it thus found a place in the confessional documents of the Protestant churches, together with the Nicene and Athanasian creeds. In the Eastern Orthodox churches the Apostles' Creed does not enjoy the same status. There the most revered of the Christian creeds is the one drawn up by the first Council of Nicaea in 325, in the recapitulated and expanded form which goes back to the Council of Constantinople of 381. The Apostles' Creed and the Nicene Creed are the most widely accepted formulations of the Christian faith in Christendom.

Baptism, faith and the confession of faith belong together in the beginnings of the Apostles' Creed. The declaration 'I believe', which is repeated in each of the three articles, means that the person who makes this profession of faith is committing himself to this God – to the Father, the Son and the Spirit. By so doing he is binding himself in solemn form. This was brought out particularly in the early church through the thrice-repeated renunciations of the devil, which went together with the creed. In response to his confession of faith, the baptismal candidate was then given over to the triune God through baptism, under invocation of the command of the risen Jesus, who is one with the Father.

Although for our modern way of thinking the creed's con- nection with baptism no longer stands in the foreground, the connection must be borne in mind if we are really to grasp properly the meaning and importance of the two words 'I believe'. For through this thrice-repeated 'I believe', the Christian today is also committing himself to God, Father, Son and Holy Spirit.

But is faith in this sense honestly possible for people today? Has the triune God not become for people nowadays a piece of doctrine surviving from Christian antiquity? How can we see in it today the expression of a reality so assured that we can trustingly give ourselves up to it? Even simple talk about God has become dubious enough for people nowadays. Does faith then need such a concrete reference and expression at all? Could not faith be trust in the future, in spite of everything that weighs on us in our present life – an 'open' trust, not one directed towards a definitely determined counterpart? But how can faith of this kind find itself reflected in the formulations of the Apostles' Creed?

Faith as the fulfilment of life is really the same thing as trust. And trust is one of the fundamental aspects of life for every human existence, going far beyond the range of the Christian creeds. Only trust allows the soul room to breathe. Every day men base their lives on an all-embracing trust, which may express itself as confidence in the particular circumstances which surround me, in the reliability of the things I deal with and, not least, in the people with whom I have to do. Even the most distrustful man cannot avoid trusting. Not of course all the time. He can refuse to trust here and there, but not everywhere and at all times.

The trust which we need to live does not only depend on definite circumstances, things or people – it forces us and carries us beyond these into what is indefinite. Hours of depression, when we are left without the life-giving breath of trust of this kind, show us especially how necessary an element of life just this indefinite confidence is. Yet this strange confidence supports everyone as long as he lives, springing up again and again beyond all doubts and failures. Thus over and above every conditional trust, with which we meet the circumstances, things and people with which we have to do, there is a deeper and unconditional trust, from which we live. But for everyone even this unconditional trust, open and unlimited though it is, depends on something. It is concentrated on some person or thing. In earliest childhood a person's primal trust is associated with his father and mother. Later this trust has to free itself from parents, but it still remains the basic condition for the formation of a healthy personality. In normal circumstances most people probably do not think much about the real basis of the trust which sustains their lives. We often only become conscious of what it is when the mainstay of our trust is shattered, thereby endangering our very capacity for living itself.

In what do we ultimately put our trust? What are our hearts set on, in the last resort? That is the most fundamental question which can face a man. 'The faith and trust of the heart makes both God and idol.' That sentence of Luther's from his comment on the first commandment is one of his most timeless sayings. And what our hearts are really set on can be very different from what we say or think is of prime importance to us. What we put our trust in, and what we do not, does not only depend on our conscious decision. Consequently the answer to the question: in whom do we ultimately put our unconditional trust? is veiled from us, and from other people. And yet we only know ourselves to the degree to which we consciously stand in the decisiveness of the trust which sustains our lives as a whole.

The openness and indefiniteness of the trust which sustains life must be consciously appropriated and taken over with conscious decision, if in the multiplicity of life's shifting situations we are to win an identity, if we want to be ourselves. As he grows up, and with the extension and clarification of the horizon of his experience, a person must become clear about where he is going to put his trust, and where he is not. Such decisions are subject to revision, but none the less what crystallizes out in them is a new definition of the substance of the trust which sustains life. This is connected with the fact that the indefinite and undefined primal trust of man demands a counterpart in which he trusts. Here everything depends on the reliability of the thing in which one trusts. For trust means reliance, and the person who relies on superficial delusions and alluring pretence is lost, as the future will prove. That is why the prophet Isaiah told Ahab, king of Judah: 'If you will not believe, surely you shall not be established' (Isa. 7.9). He meant that the man who is not anchored in what is unshakeable and enduring – that is to say in the God of Israel – cannot himself endure. For everything passes except the eternal God, and justifies no ultimate, unconditional trust.

Faith, therefore, cannot be without an object. In the act of trust a man forsakes himself and anchors himself to the thing or person on which he relies. And consequently, since man cannot live without trust, he is dependent on the truly trustworthy becoming apparent to him. For Isaiah the God of Israel was truly trustworthy; and for the early Christians, who in the words of the Roman baptismal creed repeated their threefold 'I believe', it was the God whose Son had appeared on earth in Jesus Christ and who is present through his Spirit to those who believe in him. The eternal God, who revealed his love for men through Jesus Christ, was for them the unshakeable foundation on which a man can unconditionally build.

This God is, it is true, not so unequivocal a 'datum' as the people and things with which we have to do. That is not merely a modern discovery. The Gospel of John already points out that 'No one has ever seen God' (1.18); and in so saying the evangelist is taking his stand on the Old Testament conviction that mortal man would perish at the sight of the majesty of God if this were to be revealed directly to him.

But even in other spheres of experience, what one can see is only an indication and basis for trust. Where we rely on things or people, our trust is directed towards the very thing about them which is not yet externally evident. Thus there is already an in-herent conviction in all trust that reality does not merely consist of what is visibly and tangibly present or producible. In its open-ness, which goes beyond everything that is tangibly present, trust is always already reckoning with still invisible and not yet available reality. For that is why trust can also be disappointed, and why trust and faith are always accompanied and threatened by doubt. Faith and doubt are by no means mutually exclusive; doubt is rather the shadow which everywhere follows faith and trust.

This shows that believing trust cannot be separated from the trusting person's belief in the truth of the thing in which he trusts and towards which his trust is directed. Modern theology has often made a distinction between the personal act of trust and merely believing a thing to be true. This is correct in so far as faith really does have its centre in trust and does not consist of holding this or that to be true. Mere theoretical cognizance is not yet faith, and even the acceptance of disputed information, which other people find unbelievable (such as Jesus' virgin birth, or his resurrection or ascension) is not yet faith. Only unconditional trust in Jesus and in the God whom he reveals can truly be called faith. But such trust involves believing certain things to be true; from that it cannot be separated and without that it cannot exist.

If we look at the matter more closely, we can see that believing certain things to be true is bound up with faith in three respects. *First*, it is a question of the visible indications in the existing world in which trust finds support. In the Apostles' Creed, these are above all the events of the life of Jesus, which the second article lists, but also the world of creation, to which the first article relates. *Secondly,* on the basis of these indications, trust bases itself on the invisible reality towards which trust is really directed and which manifests itself in these indications. For the Apostles' Creed this is the reality of God, the reality of his Son, now exalted to the right hand of the divine majesty, and the reality of the Holy Spirit, who is at work in the life of the church as a mysterious underlying dimension. *Thirdly,* trust is related to what it hopes for from the reliability of that to which it clings: in the creed this is the forgiveness of sins, the resurrection of the dead, and eternal life.

Trust cannot exist in any of these three connotations without truth, that is to say, without presupposing the reliability of the thing to which it commits itself. Trust cannot exist without the truth of the pointers or indications on which it rests. It cannot exist without the reliability of the invisible reality on which it depends and which manifests itself in these indications. And it cannot exist without expecting the fulfilment of what it hopes for from the steadfastness of the foundation on which the trusting person relies.

The link between trust and the proviso of faith is indicated in the Apostles' Creed by the way in which the persons of God and Jesus, whom the believer acknowledges, are more closely defined through explanatory references. Thus the God towards whom faith is directed is described and identified as the Father, as the Almighty, and as the creator of the world. The Holy Spirit is given no more precise description in the Apostles' Creed, but the Nicene Creed describes him as the giver of life, who spoke through the prophets, and who is intimately connected with Father and Son. Jesus Christ is designated in the Apostles' Creed as God's only Son, and is characterized by the whole series of statements about his earthly path down to the resurrection, the ascension, his sitting at the right hand of God, and his coming again to judgment. These closer definitions are not merely pointers designed as passing reminders of who Jesus was, without any further importance in themselves. On the contrary, for the Apostles' Creed Jesus is the person to whom faith clings only because he was crucified and rose again and will come again to judgment.

These explanatory details, by identifying the object of faith, also contain in each specific case the reason why the believer should put his trust in the person of this God, this Jesus, and in this Spirit. The confidence with which the believer trusts here particularly, and not anywhere else, has its basis in the knowledge of *what* he trusts. This knowledge will certainly remain in‚ complete and provisional and open to doubt, since it is know‚ ledge of a still invisible reality, derived from visible indications. But no trust is possible at all without a provisional judgment, based on indications of this kind, about the trustworthiness and reliability of that on which I place my dependence. And where I venture to trust without reserve, I am presupposing that the person (or thing) whom I trust in this way is capable of preserv‚ ing my existence as a whole and is ready to do so. In face of the uncertainty of human life and the doubt as to whether life has any meaning at all, and since we are dependent on trust, people are generally prepared (unless they are willing to give them‚ selves up to despair in one or other of its forms) to risk trust of this kind somewhere, in spite of all uncertainty and doubt. But sufficient indications of the trustworthiness of the thing on which the trusting person depends are none the less indispensable. Thus the Christian trusts the Father of Jesus Christ *because* he is the creator of all things; he trusts Jesus Christ *because* he has over‚ come death and grants a communion with himself which extends beyond death.

Here we come up against the real difficulties which we have

today with the Apostles' Creed and with the Christian tradition in general. For the alleged 'facts' which the creed talks about, in the second article particularly, but also in connection with the reality of God and the creation of the world (and which the Nicene Creed also mentions in connection with the Spirit as the origin of all life), are no longer undisputed. Instead of believing in the triune God *on the basis* of the creation, the resurrection of Jesus, and the activity of the Spirit in creation and prophecy, we must, it would seem, first be able to believe that these alleged 'facts' are indeed facts. Only then can they serve us as indications for a trust in this God – a trust based on them. If the Apostles' Creed has become incomprehensible for many Christians today, or is even a stumbling block in some of its formulations, this is prob´ ably due to the circumstance that the facts of redemption listed in its articles seem to have no relation to – or even seem to contra´ dict – reality as it is experienced today; and consequently they are felt to be a hindrance to present´day faith rather than the expression or primary foundation of personal faith. It would therefore seem reasonable to let the statements of the creed drop, and to withdraw to the personal act of faith, to trust in Jesus and his message of love, and in the God whom Jesus preached, the God who is love. For the ancient church, however, the love of God would have been an idle phrase without the resurrection of the dead, and trust in Jesus would have seemed groundless unless it held fast to the power of God which is present in him and was revealed in his resurrection – the God who made heaven and earth and towards whose judgment the whole world moves. If such colourless talk about the love of Jesus is to be accepted today as the way in which contemporary faith expresses itself, this is only understandable because of what still echoes through it, even if unspoken: all that the great words of early Christianity have said about the divine majesty appearing in Jesus.

It cannot be denied that the statements of the Apostles' Creed do in part cause the modern mind of the present-day Christian considerable discomfort. It is also undeniable that a number of these statements are, in one way or another, subject to considerable doubt. But it is not sensible to withdraw from the substance of these statements into an act of substantially undetermined faith, and to leave the truth of them undecided. It is not sensible because what these statements are about is precisely the primary foundation and substance of that faith. Of course it is equally impossible to establish the truth of these statements, once it has been called in question, by a flat decision to believe them. Whether the decision to believe has first to guarantee the truth of the facts on which trust in Jesus Christ and the God revealed in him depends, or whether faith is rendered independent of those facts, both come ultimately to the same thing: in both cases faith depends on the believer and this decision to believe, instead of on the factual substance in whose reliability he can trust. Where faith is understood and required in this sense – as a leap of blind 'decision' without further justification – it is degraded to a work of self-redemption. A faith which does not find its justification outside itself – i.e., from the thing on which it relies – remains imprisoned in its own ego and cannot be sustained. The reality of the God in whom the Christian faith trusts cannot be had without the so-called 'facts' to which the Apostles' Creed points and through which he is identified as this very God. Whether the Apostles' Creed has in all respects correctly described the characteristics of God's divinity and the events in the story of Jesus through which this God is revealed, is another question. To answer it demands an understanding and critical penetration into the different statements which the creed makes. The effort to understand and examine the creed's statements is the only way to be just both to its meaning for the Christian faith and to its problems; and it is the only method by which we can find a way through the doubts, instead of withdrawing to a decision to believe, which is only seemingly quite un touched by such doubts and is then always more or less forced.

Whether an examination of the truth of the statements in the creed can arrive at a final answer is, it must be admitted, doubtful from the start. Who could definitively settle the question of whether the God whom Jesus preached created the universe? Or whether Jesus rose from the dead and will also raise those who believe in him from death to his own everlasting life? Or the meaning of the Holy Spirit? Who is really capable of settling all these questions? Nobody who has become even remotely conscious of the immensity of the things concerned. But for the person who tries to discover the grounds of his Christian faith, the important thing is to penetrate so far into the ancient form ulations of the creed that their factual basis becomes accessible; then the assurance can spring up that these formulations are not simply empty phrases but point to facts which are accessible to us as well, even where we should formulate these facts differently. Once this confidence in the factualness of the transmitted credal formulae has grown up, faith can trust in the certainty of its foundation, even though this confidence will never communicate itself without any element of doubt. Faith can then presuppose the truth of the foundations which support it – even when it cannot entirely understand them and even though they may be obscured afresh through doubt. What is of decisive importance is that the believer remains aware of this premised truth as something foregiven to his faith; he cannot want to guarantee it by a decision of faith. And he must constantly ascertain the truth which he premises. At least he must be able to enjoy the confidence that it is possible to ascertain that truth, and that this is being done somewhere in the Christian church, in complete objectivity and honesty. This is what theology does, with methodological stringency. And it is only where theology does justice to this task that an atmosphere of confidence in the reliability of the Christian message springs up, in spite of all the differences of interpretation. This atmosphere is lacking today. And it is painfully missed; for it is only in an atmosphere where there is confidence in its foundations that faith can breathe freely. That is why it is more necessary today than at other times for non-theologians, too, to form their own judgments as far as possible in questions of faith.

The fact that faith lives from the truth of its foundations does not mean that it is tied to a particular state of knowledge. The results of research into the history where faith's foundations lie are constantly changing, just as our knowledge of the meaning of that history changes. This is due to the provisional nature of all human knowledge. In spite of this mutability of its results, however, Christian faith cannot do without the theological confirmation and investigation of the history from which it took its origin and which contains the foundations which sustain it. The investigation of that history, with its unique character and the implications of its meaning, shows – in spite of all the temporal conditioning of its actual form for the particular intellectual situation of the day – whether the transmitted formulations of faith are hollow, or whether, in spite of their temporal conditioning, they have a basis in fact – a basis which thereby opens up a vista towards the criteria for that unconditional trust in which faith abandons itself in order to gain a part in the thing on which it relies. No mere knowledge of the object of faith is capable of gaining a part in the saving event; that belongs to faith alone. For only in the act of faith do I forsake myself in order to anchor myself in the reality in which I trust. In this act of trust, faith goes beyond its own criteria, abandoning not only self but even the particular form of knowledge of its object from which it started, and laying itself open to a new and better knowledge of the truth on which it relies.

The formulations of the Apostles' Creed are the summing up of the sustaining foundations of the faith, which also form its central content. They speak in the language of their time, which can no longer be in every respect our language. Consequently it is not enough to recite the Apostles' Creed; one must enter into its statements enquiringly, reflectively, critically. Our way of doing this will be different from the way of the early church; nor will the contemporary Christian always arrive at the same conclusions. Can he then still repeat the early church's creed, making it his own?

It is only possible to do this responsibly if we agree with the essential intentions which found their temporally conditioned formulation in the statements of the creed. The linguistic and even the intellectual expression of these intentions can no longer always express our own contemporary recognition of the same thing. Most people would no longer of their own accord formulate many statements in the Apostles' Creed as they stand. In spite of that, we can still repeat the creed in church without doing violence to our personal sincerity as long as we are able to adhere to the intention behind its statements, critical though we may be of the form these statements take. Today the Apostles' Creed, like the Nicene Creed, is an expression of the identity of Christianity throughout the changing centuries, and over and above the widely varying interpretations of the faith. In repeating the creed we are uniting with all Christians; we are not only expressing our personal convictions. That is why it is sufficient if we share the intention behind its statements. Whether that is possible, however, demands conscientious examination. The interpretation, investigation and testing of both the Apostles' and the Nicene Creed is therefore the business of every Christian, and all the more if he is haunted by doubts about the statements of the Christian tradition as the creeds formulate them. The more or less obscure discomfort with certain formulations should not lead to the cheap way out – to the excluding of the creed from use in church and its replacement by other, supposedly more contemporary formulae, which at best could never fulfil the function of the old creeds – that through them the individual Christian can enrol himself in the communion of all Christendom. But even as regards the content of faith, nothing is gained by a change of words. What is needed is an explanation and understanding of the things of the Christian faith, which have found their expression in the ancient credal formulations. To reject these formulations simply because we find them incomprehensible is uneducated. The priest or minister especially, being trained and called to explain the traditions of the faith, should never allow himself to be swayed by this argument. It is his duty to explain the formulations which have been passed down to us. We could only justify their rejection if they had to be discarded because they were simply wrong. But today's widespread lack of comprehension of the credal formulae is a call, not for their abolition, but for their explanation. Special attention should therefore be paid in the churches to the interpretation and discussion of the statements in the creeds. Then the Christian churches will once again see the point of repeating the creed in Sunday services, as an expression of the congregation's consciousness that it is joined together with the whole of Christendom, beyond the barriers of time, in the basic substance of its faith.

In God

Not very long ago the idea that there was a God and Father in heaven was a matter of course for most Christians. This first article of faith was not even felt to be exclusively Christian; the Christian assumed that here he was at one with the majority of civilized people. The difficulties with the creed as it has been passed down to us only began with the statements about Jesus Christ as Son of God, and with the miracles of his birth and resurrection from the dead. Belief in Christ seemed to many people a troublesome addition to the simple faith in God which Jesus himself had taught.

Today the situation has been practically reversed. The world seems to have no room for a God any longer. Even theologians talk about the death of God. The only fixed point in the Christian tradition seems to be the man Jesus, with his message of love.

There are, then, theologians, too, who would like to replace faith in God by faith in Jesus. This can seem to be a bold conclusion drawn from the apparent hopelessness of the struggle about the idea of God. The defence of the idea of God can seem like a battle on the retreat and the theologians who do without it appear to be merely throwing away philosophical ballast. Would the situation of Christianity in the modern world not be made easier if we tried to do without 'the term God' in theology as well, so that Christian theology now only had to do with the existence of man? Is Jesus' message of forgiving love not largely independent of the concept of a God? And is not

the forgiving love which emanates from Jesus the real heart of
the Christian message? These are, roughly speaking, the questions
which are being raised today within Christianity itself against
profession of faith in God. Here the idea of God appears to be a
philosophical shell which has become a hindrance in our
present situation – a shell which surrounds the Christian idea of
love and from which this idea has today to be freed.

But the matter is not as simple as that. Only the person who
is all too accustomed to look at Jesus with Christian eyes can
fall a victim to the idea that belief in God can be replaced by
belief in Jesus and his message of love. Why should we go on
believing in Jesus if in him we only have to do with a man like
other men? Faith in Jesus depends on a conviction of the presence
of God in him. Only that presence lends the figure of Jesus
universal significance. Nor is the idea of forgiving love self-
supporting. Without Jesus' idea of God the message about
loving one's neighbour and one's enemy can easily appear an
extravagant demand. Sigmund Freud, for example, condemned
the idea of love as too demanding for man: 'Such a splendid
inflation of love can only diminish its value; it cannot remove
human need.' And it is true that Jesus' ethic of love must seem
to demand too much of men, if love is understood not, primarily,
as divine reality, given beforehand to all human behaviour, but
as a demand which has to be fulfilled by man. Then it must be
considered more realistic for men to meet one another with
goodwill, in so far as that is possible in the conditions of any
given situation. And for this it would hardly be necessary to
appeal to Jesus, or at least no more than to other important
teachers and models of humanity, such as Socrates or Confucius.

It is therefore not merely a curious historical fact that with
Jesus neighbourly love is intimately connected with his under-
standing of God, and indeed has its roots in that understanding.
Jesus lived entirely in the expectation of the imminent trans-

formation of the world of the present through which God will bring about his lordship and kingdom. For him the God that is to come is the all-determining reality. In the floodlight of this God's future he saw his own present. He knew himself to be sent by God, and in this mission immediately before the judgment threatening the world, he recognized the expression of the saving love of that same almighty God. His own mission to proclaim the coming rule of God counted for him as proof of the divine love, because that proclamation could bring about the timely repentance of sinners and could therefore, at the eleventh hour, open to them the prospect of the coming kingdom.

Jesus' message of love had therefore primarily to do with *God's* love, with the love of the God who was coming to judge the world that had fallen away from him. This love of God is manifested in the sending of Jesus. The Gospel of John was not the first to find the meaning of the sending of Jesus here (John 3.16); it was already Jesus' own self-understanding, as is shown by the parables of the lost sheep and the lost coin and the prodigal son (Luke 15). The love of one's neighbour which Jesus preached is nothing other than participation in God's own mind and activity, given beforehand to all human activity, and by which men ought to let themselves be possessed in their behaviour. Thus in Jesus' preaching the message of saving and forgiving love is completely and wholly founded on the certainty of God's future. To eliminate this God from Jesus' message is to take away its mainspring; and what is left is incapable of explaining either the primal prophetic force of his earthly activity or the conflict which it evoked. Moreover, without the God of Jesus, the Christian message of love would also have lost the centre from which it draws its power and authenticity.

It is therefore impossible to preserve the message of Jesus without the God of Jesus. But how can Jesus' talk about God stand up to atheism's denial of all concepts of the divine?

The key-figure of modern atheism was Ludwig Feuerbach. His book *The Essence of Christianity* (first published in 1841 and translated by George Eliot in 1853) brought a decisive break-through for his psychological explanation of religion. His lectures on the nature of religion (1846) were only a further development of his basic ideas. All important atheistic tendencies in the succeeding years have derived from Feuerbach. This is true of Marxism as well as Nietzsche, and applies to Sigmund Freud as well as Jean Paul Sartre.

Feuerbach's explanation of religion as illusion rests on his distinction between the human race and the individuals belonging to it. Whereas the individual is limited and one-sided, and to that degree finite, the race is infinite. All individual limitations of reason, imagination, will and love, will be abolished in the historical advancement of the human race. But individuals, in their narrow-mindedness and self-love, tend to see only themselves. Consequently they do not see the infiniteness of man as mankind's own fullness of being (though not the fullness of being of its individuals); instead they believe that the infiniteness of the human race is an entirely different being from man himself. Thus according to Feuerbach the idea of God arose psychologically: its *illusion* is that men hold their own nature – man's endless fullness of being as a race – to be a being alien to them. But this alien divine being is, on the contrary, in reality only *a projection* of man's own being into an imaginary heaven. Feuerbach believed that he could find confirmation of this view in the fact that God is usually thought of in analogy to man and as the perfection of everything for which man believes he is destined, but which is only realized in the life of the individual in a partial and limited way. In that man now holds his own human nature to be an alien one, he is alienated from himself. Through belief in God he denies the greatness of his own human nature. If man is therefore to find himself, he must once more recognize that what he has ascribed to an alien divine existence is in fact man's own fullness of being. Along the same lines, Nietzsche, Nicolai Hartmann and Jean Paul Sartre have demanded that we should leave every thought of God behind us for the sake of the liberty of man, human freedom being irreconcilable with belief in God.

Marx and Freud developed Feuerbach's basic ideas in a different direction. Marx deepened Feuerbach's explanation of the religious projection out of individual egoism by tracing back the religious self-alienation of man which Feuerbach described to his social and economic self-alienation, seeing it as the expression of this; Freud replaced the human race (which, according to Feuerbach, men illusorily suppose to be a being alien to themselves) by the figure of the archetypal father who, after he has been set aside by his sons, becomes the ideal of the complete power and unlimited rule which none of them will ever reach. In this way Freud, like Feuerbach, presupposes for man a non-religious primal situation. In his view that the Godhead originated in the wishes of man, he also follows Feuerbach's ideas. It is only in his account of the origin of these wishes and in his explanation of the realization of the religious illusion that he goes his own way.

The talk about the death of God so common today is also connected with the kind of criticism of religion employed by Feuerbach, or is at least linked up with it through Nietzsche. For the idea of the death of God is in fact curiously self-contradictory: a God who is no longer God could never really have been God at all. Talk about the death of God is only a mythical and pictorial way of talking about the end of the religious illusion – of talking, that is to say, about the discovery that man's notions of a God were only human dreams, the reflections of himself and his own wishes.

How does theology react to atheism's challenge? The

theologians who belong to the school of dialectical theology –
Karl Barth and, latterly, Helmut Gollwitzer – have attempted to
harness atheism for the service of a radical theology of revelation,
claiming that Feuerbach was right in exposing religion and
theistic philosophy as a human invention. It is true, they
maintain, that in religion and in the philosophers' ideas of God,
man really is only concerned with himself. But in the case of the
Christian message it is quite a different matter. That message
alone speaks of the true God. Consequently the Christian faith
is not a 'religion' at all in Feuerbach's sense.

But these arguments are not convincing. Would not every
religion have an equal right to claim an exceptional position for
its own God? And could not every religion do away with its
rivals by the simple method of declaring the other religions to be
human inventions, à la Feuerbach? There is no justification for
applying a double standard in this way. What justifies Christian
theology in detaching what it has to say about God – or what
the biblical writers have to say, or even Jesus himself – from the
context of the ideas of God held by other religions? The analo-
gies between the Old Testament and early Christian forms of
the idea of God and those of their religious environment – even
their connected origins – are too obvious to make such a
separation tenable.

The conviction that man has in general to reckon with the
activity of divine forces was one which the writers of the Old
and New Testaments certainly shared with the world that sur-
rounded them, just as did the theologians of the early church.
That belonged to the premises of their talk about the God of
Israel, the Father of Jesus of Nazareth. We only come to the
special feature of the biblical understanding of God with the
statement that the only true God is identical with the God of
Israel; and Jesus' message about the fatherhood of God refers to
this particular God of the Old Testament. Since the Christian

faith believes in the fatherly God of Jesus of Nazareth as the one true God, it also presupposes, quite apart from the divine history of Israel recorded in the writings of the Old Testament, that the question of divine reality is a reasonable one in general. When the Christian message turned to the non-Jewish world of Hellenism, beyond the borders of Israel, it was therefore able to find a point of contact in the philosophical question of the 'true' God, the true form of the divine reality. The philosophical enquiry into the truly divine became theology's ally in the struggle against popular polytheistic beliefs, since the varying schools of philosophy had already come to the conclusion that there can only be *one* God. The Christian message established its truth for the Hellenistic mind by proving itself against the criteria which philosophy had formulated as the criteria of the truly divine, which can alone be conceived of as the origin of the universe.

What is the position today? Has atheistic criticism made untenable the conviction of a divine reality which sustains man and his world – the reality whose true form the biblical tradition wanted to proclaim? In order to answer this question, we must first be clear about the general change in the philosophical question about God which has taken place in modern times, compared with the classical systems of the ancient world and their later development through the patristic period and the Christian Middle Ages. For this altered situation with regard to the question about God forms the starting point for modern atheism as well. The change in the philosophical question about God in modern times can be described as an anthropologization of the idea of God.

The old 'natural theology' of the ancient and mediaeval worlds started, broadly speaking, from knowledge of the world, going on to deduce a supreme reason as the origin of order and all motion in the world. Since the end of the Middle Ages, this approach to the idea of God has proved to have flaws. It has been recognized that the chain of causes which determine the present state of the world can very well reach back into a limit- less past, without there being any need to arrive at a First Cause: for just as in the sequence of generations, the earlier generations are carried off by death while the present generation is alive, so too could the world process in general be understood in a similar way. As long, however, as not only the origin but even the continued existence of every present state of affairs was thought to demand a cause, the assumption of a First Cause remained necessary – a First Cause which preserves the operations depending on it as long as these endure, down to the present day. Since the introduction of the principle of inertia, however, the continuance of a body in a state which has once been reached seemed to need no further explanation; and the ultimate reason for the assumption of a First Cause therefore ceased to exist. If Descartes and Newton still believed that an initial impetus was necessary for the movement of the planets, with the aim of still securing a place for the idea of God in the picture of nature, this was even in their own time no more than a faint echo of what was basically an already superseded notion. There was conse- quently something historically inevitable about the elimination of this deistic God by the mechanical theory of the origin of the planets.

Once the assumption of a First Cause for natural events became superfluous (as it did, basically, with the introduction of the principle of inertia) the approach to the idea of God via knowledge of nature was closed; but this was not true of every approach to God in general. In modern thinking, God is conceived of from the starting point of man, not from the starting point of the world. From Nicholas of Cusa via Descartes down to Kant and Hegel, the philosophers have continually shown in ever-new schemes that man cannot comprehend himself in his subjectivity without the presupposition of a divine reality. Thus for Descartes the existence of a real world outside our' selves was only assured because God existed as its author, the idea of God being discovered by the 'I' in its own consciousness without its being able to create it. According to Kant, the unity between the moral destiny of man and his existence as a natural being is only conceivable under the premise that a supreme power is concerned for the harmony between man's moral deserts and his actual fate and provides a compensation in the next world for the discrepancy existing in this. Such a being must be distinguished by moral holiness and must be at the same time able to determine the course of nature with omnipotent power. The thinkers of German idealism expanded this idea into the theory that the agreement of our subjectivity with the reality outside ourselves can only be understood in the light of the presupposition that subject and object have a common origin, different from, but including, both. Finally, Hegel showed how man is brought through his experience of the finite nature of all things – himself included – to form the idea of an infinite reality beyond himself and his world which absorbs and preserves all finite things within itself. To be more precise: the experience of finite data already contains within itself an elevation to the infinite; for we can only think of something as finite if we already have a conception of the infinite; for no limit, and nothing limited, can be conceived of without the idea of something beyond that limit. In this sense Hegel interpreted all the traditional proofs of the existence of God as being the ex' pression of man's elevation beyond the finite world to the idea of the infinite.

The same problems can be found in the present'day discussion about man, although their theological significance often only remains implicit and is not expressly called by its name. Thus W. Schulz has shown in connection with Heidegger that the existential structure of human existence draws its foundation from the being which surrounds this existence. A similar tendency can be observed in modern anthropology's talk about man's self-transcendence or openness to the world. What is really meant by describing man as a being open to the world is that man is 'open' beyond every particular form which his world takes, capable of its alteration, but also dependent on a fulfilment which the present world cannot provide. In his openness to the world, therefore, man shows himself as being dependent on a sustaining infinite reality – infinite in that it is beyond the limitations of everything that is to hand and hence is different from everything that is to hand – a reality which is the origin of his freedom, the origin of his possible elevation beyond the particular limitations of his situation.

The first and basic decision about the atheistic criticism of the idea of God as this has been developed since Feuerbach is made in the sphere of these reflections. Admittedly, it is not yet proof of the reality of God to show that it is part of the nature of man – part of the structure of his subjectivity – to presuppose a divine reality superior to himself and to all finite things, a reality which founds and sustains the whole of the finite world. For there might still be the possibility that man in his very nature is biased towards what is, for him, an unavoidable illusion. However, if it belongs to the nature of man to form the idea of a divine reality superior to the world, then it would be impossible to avoid forming this idea, even if it were an illusion. The atheistic argument, however, maintains that the idea of God can be proved to be a fundamentally conquerable illusion, which developed out of the particular circumstances of a temporary phase of human development. The heart of this argument is the demonstration that the religious theme is not necessary for a proper understanding of the nature of man. If this demonstration were successful, all further talk about God would be pointless.

If it is not successful, and if the counter-thesis holds good (the thesis that it is part of man's nature as we know it from the beginning of human history to be the religious being), this is still no proof of the reality of a God, or of his character, but the assumption of a divine reality is then certainly possible and open to discussion.

The decision about the reality of God is made in the wider context of experience of reality in general. Here we must go beyond the limitations of mere anthropological argumentation. For the assertion of a divine reality is an assertion of its power over the world and over men. Even if, as we have seen, the idea of God itself is, in the context of modern thought, no longer deducible from knowledge of the world – if, that is to say, it has another origin as an idea – its truth still depends on the power which emanates from it to illumine and elucidate the whole of man's experience of reality. At the same time, we cannot decide once and for all whether an idea of God can prove itself against experience of reality. For our experience of the world and of ourselves continually alters. These alterations are also connected with changes in the religious consciousness and with the vicissitudes of religious history. This connection does not take the form of a unilateral dependence, however; the changes in religious consciousness are not merely reflections of men's experience of the world. The history of every religion is rather an attempt to understand reality, as this is historically experienced, as being determined by the divine powers about which that particular religion knows from its traditions. Where, however, a religion's traditional understanding of God shows itself no longer capable by nature of absorbing a changed experience of reality into its understanding of the world ruled by that Godhead, it must make room for a new experience of God more capable of fulfilling this task. Intellectual and spiritual struggles and decisions of this kind stand at the very centre of the religious history of the peoples. This is also true of the history of Christianity and of the God of the Bible. The understanding of God won and preserved by the Jewish people, as it was re-modelled through the history and message of Jesus, showed itself superior to all the rival gods of the world of late antiquity through its power to illuminate and deepen that period's entire experience of reality. In the revolutionary changes in the experience of reality which have gone on for centuries, the question as far as the history of religion is concerned is: can these changes (which have been largely initiated by the section of mankind moulded by Christianity) be brought into even tension-laden accord, in the light of the Christian tradition's understanding of God, with a reality which has to be understood as a whole in the light of this God? It is only the answer to this question which can decide about the reality of the God of whom Christian tradition speaks. And every thinking person who lives in the Christian sphere of influence must find out where he stands today – whether he is confident that the God of Christianity can prove himself to be the all-determining reality, even in our contemporary experience of the world, changed as it is by modern science and its results.

The discussion about the relationship between the being of man and religion is only one aspect of this, and it is not the point where a positive decision in favour of the trustworthiness of Christian talk about God can be made. But a preliminary decision is made here; and if it is a negative one, it puts a stop to all further discussion.

The Father Almighty, Maker of Heaven and Earth

In giving the name God to the infinite reality on which man finds himself more or less clearly dependent in his nature as man, we are also describing that reality as a personal being. It is impossible to talk about gods or God without at the same time including the aspect of personality, whether one is expressly conscious of it or not. This inescapable personal meaning of all talk about gods and God is once again the occasion for the fundamental doubt as to whether any talk about God is worthy of discussion. In distinction to the atheistic argument, which took its starting point from Feuerbach, what is in question here is not the exaltation of man above everything finite (including himself) into the idea of an infinite reality; it is merely the personal character of this reality that is in doubt. At the same time, however, it is true that the argument put forward by Fichte against the personality of God became one of the starting points for Feuerbach's theory of religion, which can in a sense – namely in its theory of projection – be understood as a generalization of Fichte's.

In the dispute over atheism of 1798 Johann Gottlieb Fichte maintained that God cannot be thought of as a person without contradiction, because the idea of person includes the notion of the finite. As 'person' a being is always thought of in comparison with something else – a world of objects or other persons. The idea of the 'I' essentially and inalienably includes a 'Thou' and an 'It'. Consequently no 'I' seems capable of being everything; it always has something else as counterpart; and thus every person is, as person, limited by other things, and hence finite. In his philosophy of religion Hegel joined issue with this argument so completely that he denied the correctness of its basic concept of the person. According to Hegel, the person does not in every respect have its counterpart outside itself, as limitation of its own being; it is rather the nature of the person to be related to its counterpart, even to give itself up to that counterpart and thus to find itself in the other – in the cause which the I serves, in the thing it works on and knows, and in the Thou to which the self is bound in friendship or love. Moreover, a person finds himself again in the other in the degree to which he has surrendered and given himself up to that other. Thus in the personal life the contrast to the other, the limitation, is abolished or overcome. This shows that the person as person is, in his nature, *not* limited or finite. This is not contradicted by the fact that there are finite persons, if their finiteness is to be understood as the limitation of their being as persons. For in fact the finiteness of the human being as person is shown by the circumstance that we only partially overcome the contrast to the other – either the 'It' or the 'Thou' – and can only partially unite with it. To this extent the finite person is not a person in the full sense. The person as person, according to Hegel's ideas, would be infinite. Personality is then naturally no longer an attribute which contradicts the infinity of God.

The personal view of the infinite, of which a man as man is always aware in one way or another, is, in the form in which we meet it in religion, still far removed from the philosophical discussion about divine personality as this was carried on in German Idealism. We need not even expect to find an express concept of personality everywhere in the world of religion. Yet it is common in most religions, whether they know one god or many, for the foundation which sustains existence to be experienced as something like a person. This person-like character ascribed to the foundation of all reality is probably connected with the fact that the forces which act in events were experienced as mysterious and as not entirely comprehensible. It is true that today we think of the forces of nature as being always comprehensible and calculable, at least in principle. Consequently we no longer see personal forces at work in nature but only mechanical ones, or forces which are to this extent analogous to mechanical ones. For us, only man is still, in the ultimate heart of his being, incalculable and not at our disposal – and it is for this reason alone that for us he still counts as person. The question is, however, whether even in the world surrounding us it is not only the outward surface of events which is calculable and at our disposal; people also can be understood and manipulated in many ways. In spite of this superficial comprehensibility, however, we consider man as not being at our disposal in the depths of his existence as man. However great our psychological knowledge of him may be, as long as we are dealing with him as a man we respect the 'Thou' in him, that is to say his person. This suggests the question whether the basis of all happening in the world should not also be thought of as not at our disposal either, but as controlling us, and therefore personal. We shall return to this question later.

People experienced the power which confronted them as a will which lays claim to men, to the degree to which they found themselves confronted, in dealing with their world, with seemingly incalculable, constantly surprising forces, which were none the less not entirely without a meaningful connection and which determined man's existence. The experience of divine personality is probably based on this fundamental religious experience of power, in so far as the effects of that power (even though it is still in some degree incomprehensible) reveal that its influence on man and the world in which he lives has a certain trend. Unlike other peoples, who reckoned with a number of purposeful powers of this kind, the Israelites clung increasingly through the whole course of events to the mighty will of one single God, the Yahweh of Mount Sinai. They believed that this one God, who tolerated none beside himself, was mighty in all things. This confidence arose from their experience of this God from the time when they had committed themselves to him. And it was their experience of continually surprising and unforseeable events which led them to recognize his almighty power. By this is meant that this God is not only the origin of the present order of things, but that he is capable of every conceivable alteration, and indeed every inconceivable (for us) alteration of the present order. For him 'nothing is too hard' (Jer. 32.17, 27).

In this form the idea of the divine almighty power is specifically Israelite. It must be distinguished, above all, from every Greek understanding of God, being related rather to certain Sumerian and Babylonian deities, though these were never the only gods. It is true that in the early Greek forms of the Apostles' Creed, the acknowledgment of God as almighty is expressed through the Greek title *pantocrator*, lord of all, which was occasionally also used for Greek gods such as Hermes. But the word had long since become familiar to Jewish and Christian tradition through the Greek translation of the Old Testament, where the combination *kyrios pantocrator* was used as translation for the Old Testament name for God, Yahweh Sabaoth. This translation shows yet again, moreover, how much Yahweh's absolute power stood at the centre of the Jewish faith. The mention of the almighty power of God in the Apostles' Creed therefore brings out the identity of the God of the Christian faith with the God of Israel. The fact that for him nothing is too hard was shown anew to Christians through the raising of Jesus from the dead (cf. Rom. 4.24). God's almighty power, however, included his character as creator of all things. When the confession of faith in God as almighty ruler of all was further elucidated by the addition of an express reference to the creation of the world, this is therefore only an expansion of what was already included in the idea of almighty power. If God is indeed almighty, not only the visible world, earth, but also the invisible world, heaven, is his work.

But the unrestricted will of the God of Israel has now been interpreted by Jesus as a fatherly will. This was not an entirely new idea, but Jesus moved it into the centre of the understanding of God for the first time.

Here, too, however, difficulties immediately arise. Is the description of God as Father not an obvious reflection of a patriarchal order of society? And if that is the case, can this word still be considered the natural expression of our experience of God in the altered conditions of present-day society? In answering such questions we must first notice that the creed does not simply make the baptismal candidate state that God is his Father; it talks about the Father *per se*, namely the Father of Jesus of Nazareth. Accordingly it is not, primarily speaking, important whether we can most appropriately talk about God in relation to ourselves through the image of fatherhood; the name 'Father' identifies the God about whom the creed is talking as the God of Jesus. We must therefore ask how far in Jesus' case the name 'Father' expresses the particular character of his understanding of God.

The description of deities as 'Father' can be found in many, indeed probably most, religions. Let us confine ourselves to the more immediate religious environment of Israel. The Babylonian moon-god Sin was called the father of gods and men. The Canaanites talked similarly about their creator god El, and so did the Greeks about Zeus. The hymn to Zeus written by the

Stoic Cleanthes is a classic witness to a piety which turns to the one God as father of the universe. In the Old Testament Yahweh was only called the 'Father' of Israel in relatively late documents, from the exile onwards (Jer. 3.19; 31.9). The de- scription of him as 'Father' of the king (II Sam. 7.14) is very much older. Perhaps it was due to the decline of the monarchy that the father-relationship which, in spite of all its patriarchal superiority, at least expresses a familiar intimacy as well, was extended to the whole nation, whereas earlier the Fatherhood of Yahweh only applied to the nation indirectly, through its king.

With Jesus the idea of God's fatherly goodness and care, which is directed towards every single individual, moves into the centre of his understanding of God. Can we discover any reasons for this? At all events the naming of God as Father describes in a special way in the total context of Jesus' message the saving nearness of the God who before the coming judgment once more offers salvation to all men through Jesus – offers it, without any conditions, to everyone who has an ear for the message of the imminence of the divine rule.

Thus on the lips of Jesus the name 'Father' is no longer the symbol of the god of a patriarchal society. In the history of religion the origin of the name 'Father' for the highest deity must certainly be connected with patriarchal structures of society. But even in the Old Testament, and still more with Jesus, we are dealing with significant modifications of this symbolism; and it is these and these alone which show the specific meaning of the way in which Jesus talked about God – and hence the meaning of the credal formula, too, with its reminder of the God of Jesus whom we confess when we call our faith, faith in God the Father. On the lips of Jesus the name 'Father' indicates the particular way in which the almighty God of Israel, whose mighty coming was expected in the imminent future, has been revealed through his sending of Jesus: he is the one who wants to save men from the judgment towards which they are moving. Consequently the name 'Father' is in this particular way essentially bound up with the merciful goodness of God. That is the way in which the all-sustaining determining divine reality has been revealed through Jesus or, better still, the way in which it has revealed itself; for Jesus himself understood God as the one who was really acting in his own mission.

But how far is the fatherly God of Jesus the ultimate manifesta-tion of the divine reality with which all religions are concerned, but which still remains a matter of dispute in religious history down to the present day? For us, the Christian tradition's claim that the God of Jesus is true can only be decided, after all, once we have settled whether the God of Jesus is able to shed light on the problems of our contemporary life, and whether the reality in which we live, and which we ourselves are, can therefore be shown to be determined by him. Luther's explanation of the first article of the creed, in the Large Catechism, is along these lines: in answer to the question of the kind of God the Christian has, he replies: 'This is my God, firstly the Father who made the heavens and the earth. Other than this one God, I hold none to be God, *for* there is none other who could make the heavens and the earth.' The fact that the Christian God, the Father, has made all things and *could* make all things is, says Luther, the reason why he is the only true God. In Luther's explanation of the First Commandment the question which God is the true God remains open: '. . . it is the faith and trust of the heart which makes both God and idol. If thy faith and trust be true, then thy God will be true also; and again, where trust be false and baseless, there, too, there is no true God.' It is undoubtedly true that everyone has his ultimate trust anchored somewhere; and that that is where his God is. ('Therefore I say: the place where thy heart lies and the thing wherein thy heart trusts, that is in truth thy God.') But where, then, is the true trust, which 'finds the one true God and holds fast to him alone'? Luther answers this question in his explanation of the first article: this is the true God, because it is this God alone who was able to create heaven and earth.

This answer did not first have to be discovered by Luther. It has always been given, from the very beginning of Christian missions to the heathen and from the start of Christian theology; indeed it goes back to Second Isaiah, who strengthened the faith of the exiles by pointing out that their Yahweh was the creator of all things (Isa. 40.27ff.). But the Gentile church and its theology could more than ever believe in and proclaim the God of Israel as their God, too – and the God of all men – if they saw him as the creator of all things. That is why from the very beginning in the ancient world the Christian message entered into the philosophical question about the criteria for the true form of the divine as the origin of the world. Christian theology tried to prove itself against the arguments of philoso-phical theology because the biblical God in his Christian form had to be demonstrated against the criteria of the philosophical interpretation of the world as the true origin of all things. Although the Christian idea of God cannot be deduced from any philosophical premises, it can none the less be related to them, and demonstrates its truth in that it is sufficient for them or even goes beyond them, i.e., brings about a revision of philosophical thinking itself on the basis of philosophical argument. The fact that the discussion with philosophy took on, and retained, such intrinsic importance for Christian thinking must not be written off as foreign to the nature of the gospel; for philosophy's theme is experience of reality in its totality, and talk of God has to prove the power of its truth in the context of that theme. If God's being God means that he is the origin of everything real, and that without him there is nothing at all, then without him nothing real can be understood in depth, either; it can at most be superficially described. The discussion with philosophy must therefore show whether the God whom Christians assert can also truly be thought of as God.

God proves himself to be God in our experience of existence, undoubtedly in our highly personal experience, in every emotional crisis, in the sense of safe keeping and in the happiness of every kind that comes to us; and more especially in the sphere of moral experience. But when we limit ourselves to this very narrow, personal sphere of living, no generally applicable and tenable reason can be found why it should have to be particularly the God of the Bible who is the true God. If we take our bearings solely from the experiences of our personal life, the decision to believe or not to believe always retains an ultimately arbitrary, emotional element. It is the breadth of total experience of every and all reality which provides the field where we have to enquire whether the divine nature of the God of the Bible can stand up to verification; it is not the narrow bounds of an entirely personal experience of life, taken in isolation. The individual's personal experience of life, and his moral experience of guilt and forgiveness especially, must not be isolated; we must see it in the broad context of the experience of reality in general in which we participate as people of our own century. The individual's personal experience of life and its meaning for the verification of his faith must not thereby be, as it were, passed over or held cheap. But it must not be set apart from the total life of the time in a special enclave of pietistic devotionalism, where windows and doors are tighly closed against everything else that goes on in the world. The unity of God corresponds only to the totality of reality – reality, moreover, in its not yet concluded process. It is a unity of meaning in which all experience, even the negative experience of want, suffering, guilt and absurdity finds its place, since this unity of meaning goes beyond what is already in existence, though also embracing what is present and what has been. It has always been of decisive importance for Christianity that the God who liberates and redeems through Jesus Christ is none other than the creator of the world. All experience of redemption and liberation, however intense, remains ultimately without guarantee if in these experiences we have not to do with the creator of the world. Not only with my particular creator, as if I had to acquire through personal experience the certainty of having this God to thank for everything, and therefore of being created by him, before I could also deduce the creation of the world from the same starting-point. The process is the precise opposite: if the Christian God cannot be understood as the creator of the world, my personal experience of being indebted to him for everything can well be pious self-deception. Even the devout man knows very well that this material world is the foundation of his existence.

But, in view of the Protean nature of the totality of experience on the one hand and the limited nature of every individual's experience on the other, is it possible at all to decide whether the biblical God can be understood as the origin of all reality, as reality is to be experienced at the present day? Can we, in view of all this, maintain with Luther that 'none other could make the heavens and the earth'? There is no doubt that every answer to this question will remain a matter of dispute so long as human history has not reached that consummation which the biblical hope calls the kingdom of God. Until then there can be no final and indisputable answer to the question about the reality of God. The incompleteness of history and the incompletableness of individual experience make no other solution possible. But can no criteria be found, none the less, for at least a provisional answer?

An approach is suggested by the following observation: in the history of religion every understanding of God corresponds to a particular understanding of the world. It is impossible to associate any understanding of the world we like to choose with an equally random idea of God. For it is one function of the idea of God to determine the understanding of the world in its own light. Thus the biblical idea of God as the almighty Father also corresponds to a particular understanding of the world. This is certainly variable in detail, but it is fixed in its basic character by the biblical idea of God. We have, therefore, to ask whether the biblical understanding of reality is, in its basic character, still valid for our experience of reality, too (in so far, that is, as it is determined by the idea of God as almighty Father and to the extent to which it can be freed from certain temporally condi⁄tioned features which are not essentially and permanently bound up with the biblical idea of God itself.)

The understanding of reality which corresponds to the biblical idea of God can be characterized as a historical one. The world does not, in this view, take the form of a timeless order in which, in spite of all variation in appearances, the same thing goes on happening again and again. On the contrary: something new is always happening – something which has never been before, something without precedent, in spite of all similarity between individual events. This ever⁄new and surprising feature in events is, in the light of the almighty God for whom nothing is too hard and who demonstrates that fact again and again, the really characteristic thing about the world and man's existence. In the light of the biblical idea of God, therefore, the idea of an unvarying order cannot have the last word. That is what distinguishes the God of the Old Testament from the gods of Olympus. For the Greeks the gods were '*Seinsgestalten*', forms of being, as W. F. Otto acutely remarked. Each of them mani⁄fests one aspect of the archetypal order of the world ('order' and 'world' being in fact the same word in Greek). In Greek philosophy, therefore, it was possible to think of the cosmos even without personal gods. Israel, on the other hand, was so much overshadowed by the impression of the mutability of all things, in the light of the almighty power of its God, that even all the order which could be observed in the progress of events was bound to appear as only a contingent decree of the almighty divine will. Consequently the whole of reality was understood in ancient Israel, not as a timeless order, but as a sequence of ever⁄ new events, as a history of ever⁄new acts of God, stretching into a future which the mind could not exhaust. Furthermore, because the stress lies on the constantly contingent new event, the personal character of God could never become so colourless as it did with the Greek gods.

This might now make us entertain the suspicion that no unity at all remains in events any more if we are dealing, basically speaking, with a whole series of chance happenings. And it is true that the connection, the enduring factor, here is itself chance. But for Israel the almighty God was also the God of the covenant, who had chosen Israel and preserved it through the vicissitudes of history, just as, in being the Father of Jesus Christ, he purposes to save men from the final catastrophe and beyond it. The almighty God does not abandon 'the work of his hands'. He is faithful, holding fast to what he once did and willed. But this very holding fast takes place in continually new and sur⁄ prising ways. It is impossible ever to say positively from the standpoint of the present what the enduring things are – what will last and remain. Only the future will show what is to survive; and hence only the future will also decide what is the enduring essence of things. Thus the God of the Bible initiates the continuity and unity of the whole context of events, by returning to the past in the light of the future, holding fast to these events in his own way. By still reverting again and again, even if in surprising ways, to his initial will in every unexpected turn of events – by returning to the promises which he had proclaimed to the Israelites – the God of Israel gave the unity of history to the riot of events.

This unity only becomes visible at the end of a whole complex of happenings, running like a scarlet thread through events. It is only in the light of the end that it will be possible to decide at all what the scarlet thread is, which runs towards this end. This discovery, which can be illustrated from all historical experience, can now be generalized even further: God creates the world in the light of its latter end, because it is only the end which decides the meaning of the things and beings with which we have to do in the present. All the chances of history therefore devolve upon any given present from their ultimate future, which is, as it were, the 'place' of divine creation. Accordingly the world, and God's will with the world, and thus God himself as well, will only be revealed in the light of the end. To this extent it is highly characteristic that the God of Jesus Christ is the God whose power and kingdom are still to come and who is therefore himself still future: the ultimate and final eschatological future of the world. And it is only in the light of this ultimate future, in the light of the announcement of the coming of God to his kingdom, that the truth is unveiled – the essence of all created things, as Jesus expounded it in his parables.

Can this understanding of reality as history still claim validity for us? The questions which arise here cannot be answered in passing. We can only clarify them here to the extent of indicating the lines along which we can usefully consider and discuss them. And it cannot be solely human history which is in question, for according to the biblical belief in creation, nature, too, must be understood as 'history'.

The understanding of the history of mankind which prevails today differs from the historical design of the Bible in that it is no longer God who is the maker of history; it is man. But is this not to lose sight of the unity of man's history? The old Israelite

historians also knew that men act in history. But for them something else was involved in all human activity, something which
went beyond the intentions and acts of men. Do not events
continually take a different turn from what men plan? And is it
not this which first gives the event its deeper context? The
biblical historians at least only comprehended the path of
history when their eyes were focussed on the power which was
at work in the background of history. Historical events, therefore, seemed to them ultimately – in spite of the part played by
human activity – acts of God; and unity of meaning within the
multifariousness of historical events only showed itself to them
through God's constancy and faithfulness in all the contingency
of his actions. Modern views of history would be inconceivable
without this biblical theology of history and without the
Christian tradition. But the idea of God has been replaced by
the idea of man. Mankind is thought of as the active subject of
history – mankind realized through the individual and his
behaviour. But can mankind seriously be considered as an
active subject? The idea of history as the process of man's self-
emancipation surely has a mythological character. It rests on a
mythological exaltation of the concept of the human species.
Species do not act. That is the prerogative of individuals. The
concept of the human race cannot take over the function of the
God who acts in history. It cannot provide the foundation for
the unity of the whole of human history. This insight does not
tell us how we can justify talking about God as the unifying
subject of human history. But the theme is marked out: it is in
this setting that the question of the relevance of the biblical faith
in God for our contemporary understanding of reality can be
usefully framed and discussed.

As far as nature is concerned: it seemed in the eighteenth and
nineteenth centuries as if nature were to be understood as an
unalterable system of inviolable and eternal laws. If this were

correct, then all temporal change, all the blazing up and dying away of unique events and figures, would be ultimately unimportant for natural events as a whole – mere variations of nature's constant structure. But today one hears talk about 'history' in nature, too. The contemporary scientific world-picture is once more determined by the aspect of change – by the contingency of every individual event. Classical physics merely pushed the chance nature of the event into the background of the consciousness; it did not really eliminate it. Laws can only be observed through contingent happenings, as relatively constant processes in the stream of events, where no single happening repeats a previous one. The second law of thermodynamics has taught us to see anew that the whole process of happening in the world is irreversible. But in that case the world as a whole is a unique course of events in time, and in that case all observed regularities in events can only take place on the surface of events. Above all, however, the similarities in events, which can be described through the formulae of laws, only come into being at a particular time themselves; and the validity of natural laws too is therefore dependent on time, in so far as these laws are more than mathematical formulae – that is to say, are applicable to events in time. The relative constancy of the course of natural events is then in itself a contingent fact. At some point in the course of nature's history, the regularities within which events then proceed for an uncharted space of time have, as it were, fallen into place. And with each class of phenomena new kinds of process arise, data for the formulation of new natural laws – physical laws, for example, which only apply in the sphere of biology.

The unity of a nature understood in this way is no longer determined merely by the laws which govern its events. These laws do indeed bring out a certain similarity in the form of events: something similar is constantly being repeated. But it never happens in exactly the same form, even though the differences may be so minute that they can be ignored for the purposes of man's knowledge of nature. The idea of the complete uniformity of natural events is therefore an abstraction. It is admittedly a highly practical abstraction. It permits men to win and exert power over events to an astonishing degree. But the uniqueness of the irreversible, unparallelled course of all events cannot be incorporated in a law because the concept of law includes repeatability. If the whole unique process as something unparallelled and irreversible none the less has a total coherence, then this can only be a kind of coherence which differs from the similarities of form conveyed by a law. If one had to give a name to this coherence, which can no longer be represented by a law, one might talk about history in nature. Here, however, a final difficulty arises. We know history only in connection with historical consciousness. For us the specific historical coherence is constituted by the historical consciousness which allows all past events to be seen anew from any given present. The coherence of history does not exist at all without such glances back to the past from a given, provisional end. Every smallest unit of historical happening is already determined by its own unique form of reception of what has gone before. Since, now, nature has no consciousness, how can we talk about history in nature? It is seemingly only possible if we relate the whole process of cosmic events to man. Man, too, belongs to nature. If one looks back from man, the picture of a history of nature emerges tending towards him. But if the coherence of events of which we thereby become aware is more than a mere fiction, then it cannot be man who establishes the unity of this coherence – much less so, even, than in the coherence of human history. Historical unity is not inherent in nature. It is only recognized in retrospect, viewed from the aspect of man. But it is not based on man, either. This suggests the question of whether it is not the God of history, the God of the Bible, who is the basis of the historical unity of natural events as well.

Along these lines, and particularly under the conditions of our contemporary understanding of nature, the almighty God of the Bible can perhaps be comprehended anew as the creator of heaven and earth – as the creator of the sphere familiar to us, illumined as it is by the discovery of natural laws, and as the creator of the still unplumbed depths of events. Against the background of contingency, which determines the unique course of events as a whole, the existing inter-relationships of the natural laws appear as an expression of a divine will towards constancy, the utterance of a divine faithfulness which alone makes existence in this world possible for us. Moreover, the unity of nature, too, only finally reveals itself in its coherence (in so far as it is the coherence of a history) in retrospect, from the standpoint of God's eschatological future. The fact that this unity only emerges in a retrospective direction for the time being, i.e., from the standpoint of man (as is also shown by the fact that it is *man* who grasps the laws of events) indicates that in creation as a whole coherence of meaning, like the coherence of the history of man, is also only constituted in the light of its specific end. And this brings us face to face with the question of the ultimate end as the consummation of creation's being

And in Jesus Christ

Even the very first article of the creed does not merely deal with a general notion of God, corresponding to the questionable nature of human existence; even in these brief statements about God, the subject is the God of Jesus (the 'Father'), who is the God of Israel (the 'Almighty'). The second article focusses on this aspect of the experience of God. The God of the first article is accessible, or revealed, through Jesus of Nazareth. In this sense, the second article is, even in content, the centre of the whole creed. This is particularly clear when it calls Jesus God's 'only Son', for this gives its stamp to all the other statements in the second article. Karl Barth, therefore, maintained that, according to its substance, the second article ought really to stand at the beginning of the creed, in order to make it clear that in the Christian confession of God we are speaking of the God of Jesus and no other. But it is not the case that faith in Jesus logically precedes, and forms the basis for, faith in God. There is, rather, a curious mutual relationship between the two. This relationship cannot simply be described as a circle, either. If it has a starting point anywhere, it must be looked for, historically and in substance, in the idea of God. Substantially this starting point lies in man's being referred as man, through his consciousness of his own mortality, to an infinite reality which has always sustained him – to the dimension, that is to say, of religious experience. Historically, the starting point lies in the fact that the infinite reality which sustains the whole context of life for man and his world has long been experienced in the religions of the peoples as the operation of divine forces. The reality of God, then, was not only presupposed by Jesus, who as a Jew lived from the traditions of Israel; it was also already premised in a different way in the beginnings of the Israelite faith in God. Through the experiences which fell to Israel's lot, however, and then through Jesus, this presupposed understanding of the divine power was remodelled, acquiring a new and quite specific definition. That already became clear when we were speaking about God the Father Almighty. We are now turning to the historical figure who gave the final impress to the idea of God as this is found in the Apostles' Creed: the figure of Jesus of Nazareth.

The appeal to Jesus of Nazareth is constitutive for the Christian faith, and particularly for Christian faith in God. This will become even clearer in the course of our consideration of the statements of the Apostles' Creed. The most comprehensive perspective for Jesus' connection with God will only emerge, indeed, when we go into the statements of the third article – in the light of the theme of the Holy Spirit.

It has, however, been the conviction of Christians since the beginnings of Christian history that faith in God goes together with faith in Jesus, and can only truly be achieved through faith in Jesus. We must be clear, moreover, about the full weight of what it means to assert that a historical person, a contemporary of the Emperors Augustus and Tiberius, a Palestinian Jew belonging to the period before the catastrophe of the Jewish war of AD 70, is the criterion of faith in God for all earlier and later times. The Christian faith is founded on this historical person – that is to say, not on his teaching or anything else which can be detached from him as person, but on this particular man; and it is this which makes it so extremely vulnerable in comparison with other religions. This vulnerability consists in two things: in the first place, the question constantly arises whether the

features in the earthly activity and fate of Jesus on which the
Christian faith is based can also be judged as actual historical
facts. Secondly, the more one learns how to understand the
particular character of Jesus' historical situation, the more
pressing the question becomes how this particular historical
figure – the figure of a Palestinian Jew at the time of Tiberius,
with all the temporal limitations which that involves – can
still be for men throughout the whole twentieth-century world
the key to their understanding of existence, and therefore to their
understanding of God as well. But this vulnerability is the unavoidable reverse side of the fact which distinguishes the Christian faith from all other religions, including Buddhism and
Islam: that it is based on historical events, on a historical
figure – is based on them in the sense that they do not merely
provide the external occasion for the rise of the Christian faith,
but comprise its essential content. This differentiates the Christian message from the world of mythology, many though the
mythical elements may be which it has absorbed. But for this
reason the Christian faith is constantly confronted with the
problem how an eternal assurance and blessedness can be based
on a historical figure, and on historical events about which we
can at best claim to have probable information – information
which has, in addition, constantly altered since the beginning
of modern historical research.

We must see that this difficulty – the difficulty of building
final convictions on chance historical facts and of basing
eternal blessedness on a history which can at best only be ascer-
tained with some degree of probability – is a basic problem of
the Christian faith. It is impossible to evade it in any way at all
without losing sight of Christianity's fundamental connection
with the historical figure of Jesus. It is true that attempts have
repeatedly been made in the history of Christendom to make faith
independent of the hazards of historical knowledge. Thus Jesus

has been considered the initial historical impulse for the truths that came into the world with Christianity. Or people have believed – as they frequently still do today – that through the experience of faith they have special access to the reality of Jesus, whether they believe that they have a direct encounter with the risen and exalted one, or whether they believe that the experience of faith can mediate a particular and independent knowledge of the historical reality of Jesus of Nazareth. Or, finally, we may hear it said that the important thing is not Jesus as a historical figure, but faith in the Christian 'kerygma', in the message whose essential content consists in a new understanding of existence. All these attempts are mere flights from the fact that Christian faith rests on its connection with a historical figure and on certain historical events. They are flights from the vulnerability of Christian faith which this connection involves. But this is to surrender the fundamental relationship to Jesus. For Jesus is quite simply none other than this historical person. In that person, according to the faith of the first Christians, God himself has appeared in this world of ours, and the exalted Lord of early Christian faith is none other than the historical Jesus. That is why the early Christian message and the New Testament writings constantly point back to this historical person, and primarily to the fate which Jesus suffered – to his crucifixion and resurrection. The development of the gospel literature reveals a quite deliberate retrospective meditation on the meaning of the earthly path of Jesus. But the Pauline message, too, which seems to have made hardly any use of these traditions and concentrates solely on Jesus' cross and resurrection, held fast through these to the unique historical figure of Jesus as the foundation of faith. It is all too true that talk about the resurrection of Jesus involves uncomfortable problems for our historical thinking when we speak of it as an event on Jesus' historical path, as something which allegedly once happened at a particular time to the Jesus who was crucified. But that must still not prevent us from noting that it was the intention of early Christian witnesses to report the resurrection of Jesus as an event which once happened to this particular person and from facing up, at least, to the facts involved.

The attempts to draw up a purely dogmatic picture of Christ, independent of historical questionings, are also a flight from the problems which are bound up with the fundamental importance of the historical figure of Jesus for Christian faith. Theology cannot even remain content with the views about Jesus held by the various New Testament writings. It must enquire further about Jesus himself, behind the New Testament evidence; it must ask about his ministry and his fate if the Christian faith is bound at all to the historical figure of Jesus in its unique individuality. The question about the individuality of a historical figure and about the events which marked his life can only be presented along the lines of historical research, if we do not want to remain caught up in myths or legends, but desire really to arrive at least at the greatest attainable degree of certainty or probability. It is so important for Christianity to achieve the utmost possible degree of knowledge about Jesus, because this is the only way of protecting the believer from the danger that something may be proclaimed and believed as being the message of Christ which may perhaps have little or nothing to do with Jesus himself.

In view of these considerations, present-day research into Jesus has, since Ernst Käsemann, taken up the question of the historical Jesus once more, in contrast to Bultmann's pure 'kerygma' theology. As Gerhard Ebeling has said, Christian faith must rest on Jesus himself. Of course we must not merely take a selection of the historical facts of the life of Jesus, with the sole purpose of tracing back to Jesus himself a concept of the Christian faith gained elsewhere; the historical phenomenon of the earthly activity of Jesus and his life, death and resurrection must be considered in its whole breadth and, especially, in all the strangeness which it has for twentieth-century man. Only when we have done that can we usefully ask what abiding meaning this figure can have for us.

The strangeness of the person of Jesus, and especially the complete determination of his message and life by his expectation of the immediately impending end of the world, with which God's kingdom was to dawn – all this was brought into prominence more emphatically than ever before through the New Testament research at the turn of this century, and particularly by Johannes Weiss and Albert Schweitzer. Both the New Testament exegesis and the dogmatic theology of our century have constantly retreated before the consequences of this insight, not only because such a viewpoint is irreconcilable with our contemporary view of the world, determined as it is by the natural sciences, but also because Jesus' expectation seems to have been proved wrong by the simple fact of history's continuance down to the present day, and hence by the non-appearance of the end of the world which he awaited. It is understandable that attempts have been repeatedly made to reinterpret or to eliminate this 'eschatological' character of Jesus' message in order to preserve his possible significance for the present. But the reasons for such reinterpretation are all too transparent. Theology and Christian devotion would do better to learn how to live with the alien character of the figure of Jesus.

What can we know about Jesus? Today historical research can no longer entertain the possibility of an even relatively complete biography of him. What we have in the gospels is not, as people used to think, a connected biographical account. The sequence in which the gospels report the events of Jesus' ministry has no biographical value. On the contrary, the individual units of tradition have been put together in a quite

different order by the various evangelists, an order determined
by their particular and differing theological viewpoints. None
the less, certain important events and facts can be determined
with sufficient probability and can be viewed as historical: to
these belong Jesus' baptism by John, the basic features of his
earthly activity and message, and his death on the cross in
Jerusalem. In a sense which we shall discuss later, the resurrection of Jesus must also be included here, or at least the assertion of it by the first Christians.

Although according to the opinion of most scholars many of
the sayings of Jesus transmitted by the gospels probably do not
derive from Jesus himself, but rest on the legendary expansion of
the Jesus tradition, yet the clues we have at our disposal are
sufficient to give a picture of the character of Jesus' earthly
activity as a whole: and there is no doubt that it was decisively
stamped by the expectation of the imminent coming of the rule
of God. In face of the judgment which was approaching with
the end of the world, Jesus called for repentance, for a return to
God. At the same time, however, he could without reserve
promise the salvation of the kingdom of God to everyone who
accepted his message of its coming and at the same time recognized Jesus, its herald; or who, alternatively, accepted Jesus and
with him his message as well. Jesus could act like this because
he was convinced that the fate of men depended solely on their
attitude to the coming rule of God. This, therefore, was the
basis of the unreservedness with which Jesus was able to promise
salvation, and in this again Jesus himself apparently found the
expression of the Father's love for men. But since the eschatological hope and the behaviour which accorded with it was for
Jesus the sole criterion for participation in salvation, he was
bound to come into collision with the traditional Jewish devotion
to the Law, which saw that Law and its observance as the
criterion for future participation in salvation. That was why

Jesus was finally rejected by the Jewish leaders and delivered up to his death. But conversely, if a Jew allowed himself to be convinced of the trustworthiness of the message of Jesus' resurrection, this event was bound to mean the divine annulment of that rejection and the confirmation of Jesus and his claim that the future salvation or disaster of men would be decided before God solely by their attitude to him and to his message.

Given the premise that God himself confirmed Jesus' mission through his resurrection, it is understandable that Jesus can be called the criterion of men's agreement or non-agreement with the coming rule of God. This is so because what Jesus did was simply to face men with the personal decision for or against the future of God. If the God of Jesus is truly God and if, at the same time, Jesus has been confirmed by God in every claim made by his message, then the acceptance or rejection of Jesus' message of the imminent coming of God is in fact nothing less than the acceptance or rejection of God himself. In that case, faith in God is in fact only possible in accordance with the message of Jesus: either in the sense that a man's behaviour corresponds in practice to the criteria which Jesus preached, or in the sense that the message of Jesus is expressly accepted. The latter – i.e., faith in Jesus through faith in his message – is the way in which Jesus, as the explicit criterion of all knowledge of God, has become efficacious through the rise and spread of a community founded on faith in him.

But is trust in the God of Jesus, and therefore trust in Jesus himself as the emissary of this God, still a possibility, responsibly speaking, for men whose lives are based on the convictions of modern times? Is not the expectation of the imminent end of the world, the cosmic transformation of creation into the kingdom of God, irreconcilable with an understanding of the world which takes its bearings from the proved results of science? And has not Jesus' expectation already been refuted, in as much as the end of the world, far from having broken in on Jesus' own generation, has not taken place at all? Must we not, therefore, try to formulate the meaning of Jesus apart from this enthusiastic expectation of the imminent end, if we still want to hold fast to Jesus at all?

There are two things to be said here. In the first place, it is self-deception to think that one can separate the real heart of Jesus' message from his expectation of the imminent coming of the rule of God as the impending transformation of the world. What Jesus said about the presence of the kingdom of God during his own earthly activity is only the glare of its impending coming. Jesus' message about the love of God has its immediate presupposition in this pressing nearness of God's mighty future. For the love of God was for Jesus visible in his own mission to proclaim the nearness of the kingdom of God, both because this proclamation is God's offer of participation in the salvation of his rule, and above all because it made Jesus' unconditional promise of forgiveness possible. This knowledge of the love of God manifested in Jesus' own mission again forms the basis of his call to love of one's neighbour and unconditional forgiveness of one's fellow men – love and forgiveness whose measure is the love and forgiveness received from God himself. Because in this way the whole substance of Jesus' message has its ultimate basis in his realistic expectation of the imminent coming of God's kingdom, there is not a single word and not a single thought that he uttered which remains what it was on his lips once we take away this horizon of imminent expectation. Were we to do that, faith would no longer have anything to do with Jesus himself, but only with self-made pictures passed off under the name of Jesus.

Secondly, it is by no means to be admitted out of hand that Jesus' expectation was disappointed. For if the message of Jesus' rising from the dead can be taken seriously, it is possible to maintain that although Jesus' expectation of the imminent end was certainly not fulfilled in the world as a whole, it was certainly fulfilled in his own person. For the 'resurrection of the dead' is simply final salvation, or at least the gateway to the final salvation of eternal life, which was what Jewish expectation hoped for from the future rule of God. If this took place for Jesus, then the consummation has already dawned, for his own person at least. His claim to an authority equal to God's has then been endorsed, not by some random miracle, but by the ful-filment of the saving reality of God's rule, which he expected as imminent. This fulfilment has certainly only taken place for Jesus himself up to now. To this extent the fulfilment differs here from the promise and expectation, as it does elsewhere. But if we are permitted to take the message of Jesus' resurrection seriously, then we can no longer say without reservation that he was mistaken. And then, as Paul explained, the raising of Jesus from the dead, which has already taken place, can be a guarantee to others that the same thing can and will happen to those who are united with Jesus through faith in him, quite apart from the question of how long this world of ours is to endure.

The relevance of these considerations depends completely on an evaluation of the tradition about the resurrection of Jesus. We shall return to this in more detail later. But at the moment it can already be said that it was only through Jesus' resurrection that it was possible to believe in him again at all after his death on the cross. That was already true of the first group which gathered together after the events in Jerusalem, and it applies equally, or even more, to those of us who have come later. For the first Christians did at least share Jesus' expectation of the imminent end of the world. But today Jesus would have to be condemned as an apocalyptic enthusiast, whose thinking was completely animated by an expectation which has since proved to be an error – if the message of the resurrection did not stand in

the way. Even the Easter message must not, of course, be thus
isolated from the events which preceded it. The meaning of the
Easter event hangs on the fact that it maintains that the resurrection of the dead happened to this particular man with this
particular mission. Moreover, without the inner power of conviction of Jesus' way of talking about God, the unusual nature
of the event which the Christian Easter message asserts would
certainly occasion more scepticism about the Christian message
in general than is the case already. Yet the fact remains that in
spite of all the problems it involves, only the Easter message can
answer the challenge presented to the authority of Jesus by his
crucifixion, and for us in addition by the disappointing of the
expectation of the impending end in which he himself lived.

If, however, we presuppose that Jesus' resurrection from the
dead was the ratification of his message, then Jesus' claim has also
been reinstated, for contemporary man as well – his claim that
the acceptance or rejection of his message is the acceptance or
rejection of the imminence of God himself, and that faith in God
is not possible without a confession of faith in his, Jesus',
mission and person. The necessity for this confession of faith of
course applies only to the man who has been confronted with
the message of Jesus. It does not mean that only the Christian
can win a share in the divine salvation. In the beatitudes Jesus
called blessed the suffering, the weak, the merciful and peace-
loving, the people who hunger and thirst after righteousness and
those who suffer for righteousness' sake, quite apart from their
relationship to him. Anyone who lives in such a situation,
anyone who is not overcome by his suffering and his helpless-
ness, anyone who truly strives after greater righteousness and who
is filled with the spirit of mercy and peace is trusting, practically
speaking, in the God whom Jesus preached. Thus far the
message of Jesus is the criterion for *his* participation in divine
salvation as well.

In that Jesus is the criterion for the relation of all men to God, even those who have never encountered him, he is himself one with God. This bond with God and with the cause of God in the world was expressed by the early church through the titles which they conferred on Jesus. They saw in him the Son of man of Jewish expectation, who was to come in the clouds of heaven to judge the world. They saw him as the prophet promised for the end time, but also as the suffering Servant of God. And they found in him the promised Messiah, the Son of God.

The word Messiah means 'the anointed one': the Greek word is *Christos*. In the way in which it is used in the text of the creed, this word has long since been turned into a proper name, a part of the name Jesus Christ. Originally, however, 'Messiah' was a title, borne by the ancient kings of Israel. The king was accounted the one anointed by God *per se*, and even during the period of the kings of Judah the hope of a future king grew up, a king who would perfect the king's function of ruling in the name of God over Israel and the world in peace and righteousness. But there is no unbroken connection between this hope and Jesus. On the contrary, it seems probable that Jesus expressly rejected the title of Messiah which was offered to him. In its original form the tradition about Peter's confession (Mark 8.27–33) may have amounted to a still brusquer rejection of the title of Messiah on the part of Jesus than the present text indicates. To be turned into the bearer of the national hopes of the Jewish nation was evidently viewed by Jesus as a temptation of Satan. For he was the very contrary – the herald of God's rule as the imminent end of all worldly political organization. The nation was to turn to this future, to the kingdom of God breaking in from eternity, instead of clinging to its hopes of national restoration.

Although Jesus rejected the title of Christ for himself, it was later assigned to him. Is this justifiable? First we must understand how it came about. Among the Romans Jesus was apparently accused of being a political agitator and was executed as such. The reason for his execution was stated on his cross: he wanted to be 'king of the Jews' (Mark 15.26). The mention of the inscription on the cross in the gospels is today once again judged by many scholars to be a piece of historical information. The association of the title Messiah with Jesus, which is brought out in the inscription, was wrong in so far as Jesus did not lay claim to that title, as we have seen. Yet this association became Jesus' destiny. Certainly, that is not enough to explain how the community of his disciples was able to see Jesus as the Messiah, contrary to what he himself said. But here one must remember that after the resurrection there was no longer room for any bringer of salvation apart from Jesus, whose second coming the church now awaited. Consequently Jesus was now viewed as being identical with the end-time figure of Jewish expectation – with the Son of man, about whose coming he probably talked himself; and with the Messiah, with whom, against his will, he had become indissolubly linked through his fate. His church was now able to see in him the true Messiah. The Messianic ex-pectation was thereby changed from a hope for the fulfilment of existence in this world into an expression for the reconciliation of men which overcomes death, a reconciliation beyond this world through Jesus.

The justice of calling Jesus the Messiah, or Christ, therefore lies in the fact that no other bringer of salvation was now to be expected, so that all men's expectations of salvation could be transferred to Jesus, since the aspects of truth which those ex-pectations possessed were fulfilled in him. Ought, perhaps, the concept of Messiah to have been avoided, in face of Jesus' own rejection of it? The question is a justifiable one. But the bringer of salvation whom the Jewish people expected in the figure of the Messiah was, after all, actually Jesus, even if in a different form from what the Messianic hopes had imagined. Once the danger of misunderstanding his mission through the stamp of the title of Messiah had been overcome (a danger which Jesus warded off by his rejection of the name), that title could, conversely, be transformed through its transference to Jesus, the one who was crucified and rose again from the dead.

The special feature of the title Messiah, as distinct from the other early Christian titles which were applied to Jesus, such as Son of man, Son of David, Lord, etc., is that the concept of the Messiah was capable of absorbing into itself the whole diversity of Jesus' significance. In the first place it designated the future function of Jesus at his second coming, when he was finally to set up the rule of God. Then, it could also be related to the present reality of the risen Lord, who already rules over the world in hidden fashion at the side of God. The inscription on the cross further made it possible to associate Jesus' sufferings with his Messianic dignity as well, and thus to see the earthly Jesus as already being the Messiah. But the elements of the mediation of salvation and of divine sonship were also associated with the title Messiah; and these elements became of decisive importance for the proclamation of the significance of Jesus in the world moulded by Hellenism – that is to say, in the early church's mission to the Gentiles. Thus the title 'Christ' could be transformed to such a degree that it finally embraced the whole fullness of meaning found in the person of Jesus, his earthly activity and his fate. It is therefore understandable that for the Jewish missionaries of the early Christian period the name Messiah could become the quintessence of their whole message about Jesus – as it did for Paul, for instance. And this was particularly the case when they turned to the Gentiles, going beyond the borders of the Jewish tradition. For Gentile hearers of the message, however, to whom the titular meaning of the designation Christ was less familiar than it was to those who had been born Jews, the word became a component part of Jesus' name.

Finally, we must bear two points in mind:

1. The name Christ especially signifies Jesus' importance for salvation. It brings out expressly what already emerged as the conclusion of our question about the historical Jesus: that he claimed to implement God's decision about men by forcing them to decision as regards his message about the divine future; and that this claim was confirmed through his resurrection from the dead, but in such a way that in the name of Jesus salvation, future communion with God, participation in the new life which appeared in his resurrection – all this is opened to all who believe in Jesus and put their trust in him. This significance for salvation is not attached to Jesus from outside, as if it might just as well be ascribed to some other figure. It is part of him; it emanates from him. But that is not self-evident when we talk about Jesus. The power of salvation which dwells in him and emanates from him must be expressly designated as such; it must be given a name: that is why we talk about Jesus Christ. By confessing Jesus as Christ we are saying that our life only takes its meaning from him, only becomes a whole – only becomes *whole* – if he is the focus. This means that our existence viewed in isolation is not 'a whole' or 'whole', although it is the longing of every man that it should be. So much in life towards which our destiny drives us remains unfulfilled. So much begun is broken off; and what takes form is distorted by necessity, or indolence, or error. In the end everything, even the most completely fulfilled life, remains a fragment, which death leaves as an open question. But through his death on the cross Jesus communicated the nearness of God, in which he himself lived, in the most extreme situations of failure which life can bring.

This nearness of God does not appear in the fulfilment of earthly life, nor does it end with life's failure. If at all, our existence can only become 'whole' through fulfilment in the next world. That does not mean flight from this world into something outside our lives. On the contrary, it means living *this* life in trust, in the wholeness of our being. This wholeness is not clearly present in the present reality of our lives, and only shows itself in fragmentary form to the person who is capable of seeing the whole in the fragment; but it is promised and guaranteed by Jesus' message of the future of the kingdom of God and by his resurrection from the dead. From this starting point even the situations, experiences and opportunities of our present life can be lived and experienced as a part of the whole which they cannot of themselves substantiate.

2. The confession of faith in Jesus as Christ does not only mean that we put our trust in Jesus, and that in his light our lives can be 'whole', can be lived as a whole. Confession of faith in Christ also carries with it the bond between Christian faith and the history and hopes of the people of Israel. These hopes, as we have seen, were changed by Jesus, not only because he first rejected them, but even more because they have none the less been linked with him. The content of the idea of Messiah changed radically, moreover, compared with the extent to which Israel's understanding of God, for example, was altered by the message of Jesus. In spite of this a continuity remains, a connection which alone makes the transference of the title 'Christ' to Jesus meaningful and which in fact also made it possible. Although the title Christ took on a new meaning in the course of its transference to Jesus, the early church still believed that through it they could proclaim Jesus as the fulfilment of the Jewish Messianic hope. And it is only in the light of the Jewish Messianic hope that the saving significance inherent in the person of Jesus could be perceived and expressed in all its fullness. Without this context of expectation, an essential part of the meaning of the historical Jesus would probably never have

been realized. So in this respect, too, the Christian church has become the heir of Israel's history of faith; and it must remain conscious of this heritage if it wants to preserve its awareness of the fullness of meaning of the person of Jesus and his life, death and resurrection.

God's Only Son, Our Lord

The profession of faith in Jesus as Son of God is for many people today one of the statements of the church's tradition which is particularly difficult of access. For that very reason other people see this statement as being all the more the decisive criterion of true faith. Both parties are thereby treating this talk of Jesus as Son of God as the assertion of Jesus' supernatural nature. They differ only in that the one party clings to this assertion whereas the other party rejects it, or at least takes a sceptical view, finding in it a mythological heightening of Jesus' simple manhood. For these people the idea of the divine sonship seems to make it basically impossible to understand Jesus as a man like ourselves. But the notion of a supernatural being merely dressed up, as it were, in the human form of Jesus, seems irreconcilable with any interpretation of reality which could be maintained today.

Such a sceptical view of the early Christian title Son of God can certainly not be reproached with completely failing to grasp the concept of the divine sonship of Jesus prevailing in the Christian tradition. On the contrary, we must judge it to be in this respect largely accurate. But it is as unjust to what was originally meant by calling Jesus the Son of God as the traditional point of view which it rejects. The motives which have found their expression in the use of the title are being disregarded, if one only has in mind what I have indicated as the traditional way of thinking of the Son of God as a supernatural being. For it is actually possible – and indeed historically and exegetically

necessary – to understand the title Son of God as being the
interpretation of Jesus' *human* appearance. This interpretation
had its own history in the primitive church. If one starts from
the New Testament texts in their final form, one can trace a
number of different stages in the development of the Christian
conviction of the divine sonship of Jesus, going back to Jesus
himself. Moreover, it is possible to deduce the impulses which
found their expression in the formula that calls Jesus the Son
of God. It is then possible to see that the changes in the
understanding of the formula were not simply arbitrary, either;
we can see that they were prompted by the subject-matter itself –
that is to say, by the unique nature of Jesus' earthly activity and
his life, death and resurrection. For it was the unique meaning of
these which was at stake in the history of this interpretation.

At the beginning, the name of 'Son' for Jesus was extremely
closely connected with the idea of God as Father. The title 'Son'
was, so to speak, the reflection which Jesus' proclamation of
God as Father threw back on the proclaimer himself. For it was
by no means a matter of course to talk as intimately as Jesus did
about God as Father. On the contrary, it was part of the special
character of Jesus; and it was the special way he talked about
God which seemed to set him apart from other men, even to his
disciples. This is most clearly expressed in the gospels through a
group of sayings in which Jesus is simply called 'the Son'. This
appellation can be explained most easily by the fact that Jesus
proclaimed God as 'the Father'; and his church accordingly
called him 'the Son'.

The title Son of God had another connotation, although of
course to talk simply about Jesus as the Son also meant that he
was the Son of the Father: thus the transition to the title Son of
God is understandable. But this title was already a traditional
one. It is closely related to the title Messiah. In the Jewish
coronation ceremonial, of which a fragment has survived in the

Second Psalm, we read that Yahweh says to the king (the anointed one): 'You are my son, today I have begotten you' (2.7). This can hardly mean that the king is physically descended from Yahweh, in the way that the Egyptian kings of the Middle and New Kingdoms were thought to be sons, in the physical sense, of the god Re. What we have to do with in the Second Psalm is an act of adoption. As Yahweh's son, the king assumes Yahweh's rule over the world, on his behalf (Ps. 2.8; 110.1).

These ideas were transferred to Jesus in the primitive church: in Rom. 1.3f. Paul quotes an already existing credal formula according to which Jesus was designated 'Son of God in power' through his resurrection from the dead. Here the resurrection counts as the point in time when Jesus was appointed to the divine sonship, as the time of adoption. In another, probably later tradition, this moment was set back to Jesus' baptism. Thus according to Mark 1.11 the saying in Psalm 2.7 was pronounced over Jesus at his baptism by a voice from heaven. Here, therefore, Jesus was understood as having been already installed as Messiah at the beginning of his public ministry. In the legend of Jesus' virgin birth we have to do with a further stage in this development: it takes back the origin of the divine sonship even further, to Jesus' birth. Luke (1.35) expressly explains the title Son of God as meaning that Jesus had no human father apart from God. The motive behind the process of building up a tradition which thrust the origin of Jesus' divine sonship further and further back is obvious: its intention was to express the idea that Jesus was the one to whom God has delegated his rule and the exercise of his will from the very beginning. This motive corresponds to the fact that Jesus' resurrection confirmed his pre-Easter claim; that is to say, it was his subsequent but retrospective legitimation.

The title Son of God did not therefore originally signify

physical sonship, nor did it mark Jesus out as a divine, supernatural being: after all, the king of Judah, who was addressed
as 'Son of God', certainly remained a man. In the Jewish sphere
of tradition the title Son of God merely characterized Jesus'
function – that he had been appointed to exercise God's rule
over the world; it did not describe his nature. This altered in
the Hellenistic world of ideas. There the title Son of God
became the term for a superhuman or divine being which
'appeared' in Jesus, the man, but which was distinct from him.
We are told that this divine being was 'sent' into flesh so that he
could assume human form. This is the way in which Paul
already expressed it in Rom. 8.3 and Gal. 4.4. The Apostles'
Creed also undoubtedly understands the expression Son of God
in this way: as a pre-existent divine being (i.e., a being already
existing in the eternity of God before Jesus' earthly birth) which
at Jesus' birth took on human form and human existence.

Before commenting on this idea of pre-existence, let us first
consider the particular nuance which the Apostles' Creed
associates with the idea of Jesus' divine sonship. It calls him the
only-begotten Son of God. In the New Testament this term
expressing the relation of Jesus to God is only used in John. It
means that Jesus is God's *only* Son. Apart from him God has no
other son, no other deputy and plenipotentiary in his kingdom.

As the sole representative of God's rule in the world, Jesus is
also the mediator of its creation. In the Nicene Creed the
declaration of the divine sonship of Jesus Christ is expressly
linked with the statement that through him 'all things were
made'. This idea is understandable if Jesus as Son of God
exercises God's rule over the world. Here certainly we do not
have to think of a divine being entirely separate from the historical
Jesus, with some particular function or other at the beginning of
the world. On the contrary, Jesus Christ is the mediator of
creation *in so far* as he can be called the Son of God, and in the

same way. Let us recall here the idea we touched on earlier, that creation took place in the light of its end. Jesus is then to be understood as the mediator of creation in so far as he is the end of all things and inasmuch as the end of all things has already appeared in him – the end which decides creation's true nature. Because it is he who brings the end, all things tend towards him, and because they tend towards him, they also take their bearings from him. Jesus is therefore the representative of God's rule over the world, in so far as he is the centre, or rather the end, of history, thereby being the mediator of creation. This statement brings out the all-embracing importance of what has happened in and with Jesus. And that is also the meaning of the phrase about Jesus being the one, only-begotten Son of the divine Father.

Because Jesus is the only-begotten Son of God he is also the sole bearer of the divine revelation: no-one knows the Father except the Son and any one to whom the Son chooses to reveal him (Matt. 11.27; cf. John 14.6). For that reason the revelation of God is also in the fullest sense of the word a single revelation, the revelation through his only Son.

To arrive at a theological recognition of this we must admittedly trace the chain of argument in the reverse direction: in actual fact the revelation of God in Jesus and its unique nature may be founded on his being the only-begotten Son; but for us, for our way of perception, talk about Jesus as the only Son of God is, on the contrary, only an expression of the fact that God is revealed in him. There are, it is true, many self-manifestations of the divine reality from which human life has always taken its bearings. For in fulfilment of their existence men do not only presuppose this reality, which sustains their own being and the being of the world; they are always in the process of dealing with it in one way or another. The divine reality manifests itself to men in many ways in intercourse of this kind, and the history of religion is full of the traces of such manifestations. But there is generally something provisional about them; they can be replaced by other, new experiences of the same reality. For that very reason they have not the finality of a divine self-revelation. Even where they come forward with the claim to sole and final truth, they lose this character again in the new experience of God which replaces them. Jesus' message about God, however, is final in a quite unique way, not in the sense that we are assured that it is final, but because of the unique character of its content, since Jesus proclaimed that the only essential thing for men was to trust in the divine future. Consequently his message cannot be superseded by any divine future self-revelation. Jesus was there- fore able to anticipate God's final decision about men, and could preach God's judgment or his forgiveness according to men's attitude to his message. It was through his claim to this final 'eschatological' authority that he raised the opposition which finally led to his crucifixion. In the experience of his disciples, however, his authority was confirmed by God through his resurrection from the dead – that is to say through the appearance in Jesus of the last, final reality of life from God. In this ultimate validity, that is to say because of its 'eschatological' character, Jesus is, in the sense we have described, the revelation of God. Consequently we can understand the early Christian formula and make it our own when it says that Jesus is *the* 'Son' *per se* of the God whom he called Father. For in Jesus' proclama- tion of the future of God as being alone decisive for the salvation of every man, the future of God already took up its rule in the present, wherever men listened to his message. Consequently, with his announcement of the future of God and his proclama- tion and practice of the love of God for men which was based on it, Jesus is the representative of the divine future among men; and he was finally confirmed as such when God raised him from the dead. As the bearer of God's final self-manifestation and as the one who, by virtue of this mission's authority, already anticipates God's final decision about men and the world, Jesus can also be accounted 'the Son', the only Son of this Father.

At the same time it is well to be conscious that this is a figurative, metaphorical way of speaking. The formula Son of God does not originally point to Jesus' supernatural physical descent. It serves to interpret his relationship to the God he proclaimed, the relationship which came to expression in his mission and his life, death and resurrection. The pictorial expression 'Son' is a completely comprehensible and appropriate way of describing this, especially when we think of its Old Testament origin. We should not perhaps choose it directly ourselves, as the expression of our own experience, any more than we would choose the name of Father for God. But then we are not faced with such a choice – as if no expression for the person of Jesus had as yet been found in the history of the Christian faith, so that Christians had to begin completely afresh today. It would be an illusion to behave as if one could always start from zero. Every Christian today enters into a history of faith in Christ which is at the same time largely the history of the interpretation of the person of Jesus. This does not mean that he has to be uncritical towards the tradition, but as a Christian, however critical his attitude, he will so behave that he finds his place within that tradition. Consequently he can neither ignore the fact that Jesus talked about God as the Father, nor that the church of Jesus as a result understood him as 'the Son'. Moreover this step can stand up to examination even today as being essentially justifiable. It is true that the figure of Jesus as the 'Son' appears in a different light to this contemporary understanding from the way it appeared to the first Christians themselves. The fact that the title was already bound up with the interpretation of the person and life of Jesus in the primitive church has a basic significance for the meaning of the title in our understanding today. For fitting the living into the history of the tradition always means relating to the present what has been passed down; and with this, history itself turns into a dimension of present experience. That becomes evident, in this case, in the fact that a Son of God, or anything of the kind, is for us no longer *per se* a plausible figure of the supernatural world; it is only accessible to present-day understanding in the context of the interpretation of Jesus' human reality.

As the revealer of God, Jesus is 'the Son'; and he belongs so closely to our knowledge of God as God that we can no longer think of that Godhead adequately apart from Jesus. For it is through Jesus that the divine future becomes present reality. By sending Jesus, God shows the love which is his nature. In this degree Jesus himself is an inseparable part of the Godhead of the eternal God, although he only appeared late in the world process and the process of human history.

This man's essential relationship to God's eternal Godhead leads to the idea of Jesus' pre-existence as Son of God, an idea which we already find in Paul (Rom. 8.3; Gal. 4.4). If we seriously mean that Jesus, as the person through whom God is revealed, belongs to the very essence of God himself, then he must in this respect – in respect of his unity with God – have already been the Son before he became man, before his human birth. The assertion of Jesus' pre-existence as Son of God is therefore nothing more than a conclusion drawn from Jesus' unity with God himself in his revelation. It includes Jesus' oneness of nature with God. For otherwise God would not be revealed as himself in his revelation in Jesus. But Jesus' oneness of nature with God also means that this man participated in God's eternity, although he was, as man, not eternal but born in time, like the rest of us.

That as the Son of God Jesus belongs to the essence of God himself is also brought out through the term 'Lord'. It is the substance of one of the oldest Christian credal formulae which the early Christian tradition preserved. Thus in Paul (I Cor. 12.3) we read: 'No one can say Jesus is Lord except through the Holy Spirit.' The word Lord, Kyrios, is used in the Greek translation of the Old Testament as a paraphrase for the Old Testament name for God, Yahweh, which the devout Jew avoided pronouncing. Jesus may perhaps have been called 'the Lord' before Easter, in the more commonplace sense of a polite form of address. Later this custom merged, at least, with the weightier meaning of the word 'Lord', as a paraphrase for the name of God, because in Greek both meanings are expressed through the same word, Kyrios. This process, and the resulting address of Jesus as Lord in the divine sense, was substantially justified by the fact that Jesus, as eschatological herald, the revealer of God, is the Son of God and so is one with God himself. It is probable that the title Kyrios brought out this unity definitely for the first time in the history of the early church, even more clearly than the title Son of God. For to Jewish understanding the latter still primarily contained the idea of subordination to God. The function of representing God's rule on earth did not necessarily break through the limitations of creatureliness. It was in the Hellenistic sphere that the Son of God was first understood as a divine being. At the same time this understanding is, as we have seen, already present in Paul. Here the idea of the divine sonship of Jesus moved for the first time into immediate proximity to that unity with God which is expressed in the title Kyrios. This development, too, must be judged as being essentially justifiable, however, if the sonship of Jesus is understood as the expression for the final character of God's self-manifestation through Jesus, which in its finality includes the aspect of oneness of nature.

Ultimately, therefore, the acknowledgment of Jesus Christ as Lord is closely related in substance to belief in him as Son of

God. Yet the two statements have from a purely linguistic point of view an emphasis which is the complete reverse of the different meanings which the two bring with them from the history of the tradition. Taken literally, the title Son of God describes primarily and expressly the relationship of Jesus to God, to the Father, and only implicitly his position with regard to the world. Conversely, the title Kyrios, Lord, seems primarily to express this relationship to the world in the sense of rule, whereas Jesus' unity with God, his relationship to him, is only implicit in the title and has first to be worked out through a consideration of its proper and original meaning. Yet the Apostles' Creed apparently already understands the two titles in this sense when it talks about Jesus as *God's* only begotten Son, but *our* Lord. In this way it describes Jesus' relationship to God on the one hand, and on the other his relation to us and to the world, as this is founded on the first.

As 'our Lord', Jesus was opposed in the faith of the early Christian church to the numerous 'lords' known to the Hellenistic world – on the one hand the Roman emperors (who were given the title *kyrios* in Greek), and on the other the gods of the mystery religions. In contrast to all these, Jesus Christ was proclaimed as the true Kyrios, the true Lord of the world. Everything was to be subjected to him. For that reason the missionary task of the church particularly stands under the token of Jesus' dignity as Kyrios. And for the same reason, since the early period of Christianity, the title Lord has signified the claim of the proclamation of Christ to universal, all-embracing truth – truth which proves itself by its capacity for absorbing all other truth into itself.

Conceived by the Holy Spirit, Born of the Virgin Mary

In the Roman baptismal creed of the third century this formula still ran: born of the Holy Spirit *and* the Virgin Mary. The two parts of the formula stood side by side, whereas in the present version what comes from God (conceived by the Holy Spirit) and what comes from man (born of the Virgin Mary) are set over against one another. Otherwise the sense is the same. Jesus' existence has its foundation in God – it takes its origin from the Holy Spirit; and yet he is also born of Mary in a truly human fashion. For curiously enough, in the church of the first centuries the virgin birth counted as being the special token of Jesus' true humanity, in opposition to the Gnostics, who did not want to allow the Redeemer a truly human birth and either made the Son of God live among men with an apparent body, or thought that he was only seemingly united with Jesus the man. In either case the idea was that the unchangeable God could not be truly one with a changeable, suffering and dying man, born in time. Contrary to this view, the creed stresses with the 'anti-Gnostic' fathers of the second century that the Son of God himself was born through Mary. There was not such stress on the virgin character of this birth as is the case with our own contemporaries, who are put off by this particular point. The virgin character of Jesus' birth rather counted as a matter of course: for Jesus, as Son of God, not to be born like other men could seem highly plausible to people of the Hellenistic period. After all, the pagan myths also recorded the divine origin of important men and great heroes – Perseus and Hercules, for example, who were the sons of Zeus. And why should Jesus be inferior to the great men of ancient Israel who were chosen 'from birth', like Samson (Judges 13.5), Jeremiah (1.5) and the Servant of God (Isa. 49.5)? Did not Isaiah proclaim the birth of the Messiah through a virgin? This at least was what could be read in the Greek translation of the Old Testament (Isa. 7.14 LXX, quoted in Matt. 1.23).

Today the assertion of Jesus' virgin birth seems, rather, to be a diminution of his true humanity. Nor can we see any longer why Jesus as Son of God should come into the world in a different way from anyone else. Above all, however, there are strong historical objections to the tradition about Jesus' virgin birth, and since this tradition is in the nature of a factual assertion about a past event, historical objections cannot simply be set aside.

The tradition about Jesus' virgin birth only appears in two of the New Testament writings, in Luke and Matthew. Paul and John expressed themselves more or less clearly in the opposite direction: in Gal. 4.4, Paul said that the Son of God was born of a woman and subject to the Law. His intention in saying this was to bring out Jesus' similarity to other men, whereas the original purpose of the tradition about Jesus' virgin birth was to establish his very difference. A particularly important point is that Paul was certainly familiar with the idea of a miraculous birth. He mentions it in connection with the birth of Isaac through Sarah (Gal. 4.23, 27, 29); but he applies it, *not* to Jesus, but in an allegorical sense to Christians as heirs of the promise (Gal. 4.28). If these comments make it seem improbable that Paul was even so much as familiar with the idea of Jesus' virgin birth, there is a phrase in the Gospel of John which must perhaps even be construed as a polemical allusion to the tradition. For in John 1.13 we are told immediately before the sentence about the incarnation of the word (1.14) that Christians in general are born 'not of blood nor of the will of the flesh nor of the will of man, but of God'.

Of the two texts in Matthew and Luke, which are the only ones to pass on the story of Jesus' virgin birth, Luke 1.26–38 is the earlier. The point of departure for this story emerges in the phrase that Jesus was to be called the Son of God because he was created from Mary through the creative Spirit of God himself. This sentence gives us the key to an understanding of the whole story. For it means that we have to understand it as a picture and explanation in concrete terms of the title 'Son of God'. The story is to explain why Jesus is called the Son of God. But since this title is much more widely distributed in the early Christian tradition than the story of Jesus' virgin birth, and since other reasons for this title are given in other texts (where it is traced back to Jesus' resurrection or his baptism), our story can only be considered as a retrospective explanation of the title which had already been conferred for other reasons. A story of this kind is known as an aetiological legend (or saga) because its purpose and motive is to explain how a certain state of affairs has been arrived at – what its *aitia*, or reason, is. In this case the already-existing state of affairs which forms the subject of the explanation is, as we have said, the application of the title 'Son of God' to Jesus. The investigation of the tradition itself in its earliest form therefore presents us with the strongest argument against its historical reliability, in that it shows its own point of departure and motive.

So in the virgin birth we have to do with a legend. That can be asserted in this case with complete certainty, because the transmitted text itself shows so clearly the motive for the legend-ary rise of the tradition. That distinguishes the story of Jesus' virgin birth fundamentally from the traditions about his resur-rection, with which it has often been compared. Karl Barth, for

example, has spoken of the two miracles at the beginning and
at the end of the story of Jesus. Such a comparison is completely
wide of the mark. Naturally one can ask whether there are
legendary elements in the resurrection traditions as well. But
there it is never possible – as it is here – to show the motive from
which the whole tradition could have developed. The development of the resurrection tradition, although it contains a number
of supervening legendary expansions, is in general only comprehensible from historical points of departure, which form its
substance. The tradition of the virgin birth, however, obviously
developed as a whole out of the motive of explaining the title
Son of God, which had already been conferred for other reasons,
as the earliest transmitted version of the text expressly shows. A
similar demonstration of the origin of the Christian Easter faith
has never been attempted, even by its severest critics. For the
Easter tradition offers no jumping-off point for an explanation
of this kind. That is the fundamental difference in the form of
the two traditions and in the process of their transmission. This
goes with a similar fundamental difference as regards their
importance for the Christian message. For the Christian message
apparently existed for the most part in the primitive church
without the notion of Jesus' virgin birth – if the idea was not
even deliberately rejected. But there has never, from the very
beginning, been a Christian message which is not essentially a
message about the resurrection of Jesus from the dead. This is
the sustaining foundation of the whole Christian proclamation,
whereas the story of the virgin birth is marginal in comparison.

We must still go rather more closely into the reason for this
legend. It is already clear that it explains the title Son of God.
But since the legend still has its roots in the sphere of Jewish
Christianity or, more precisely, in a Jewish Christianity stamped
by Hellenism, we can hardly suppose that the people who first
related this explanation of the title Son of God were not aware of

the title's older meaning, according to which the divine sonship by no means required a supernatural birth. We must therefore assume that the first people to tell the story of Jesus' virgin birth were thereby consciously intending to give a new interpretation of his divine sonship: the theological intention of the story lies in the implication that Jesus did not only become Son of God through his resurrection, or only after his baptism by John: he was the Son of God from the beginning. In spite of all that we have said up to now about the legendary character of the story of Jesus' virgin birth, we are bound to see in this theological intention the aspect of truth which the story contains. The intention to show that Jesus was the Son of God from the beginning is particularly justified, moreover, in the light of Jesus' resurrection, since this not only meant the confirmation of his pre-Easter message, but also the ratification of the claim as regards his own person, which was inevitably linked with it – a ratification which consequently reacted retrospectively on the origin of that person.

This theological intention, as we mentioned earlier, led in the early church to the idea of the pre-existence of Jesus. For the raising of the one who was crucified confirmed Jesus in his unity with God. And that means that in his mission and in his person Jesus was one with the eternity of God, even before his human birth.

The idea of pre-existence was in later times associated with the virgin birth within the notional framework of the incarnation of the pre-existent son of God. The idea of incarnation finally sums up what Christians have to say in the light of the Easter faith about the presence of God in the person of Jesus. Belief in the incarnation is even connected with the message of Jesus himself; for Jesus talked about the coming God's presence in his own earthly activity and in what he said and did. Belief in the incarnation is the form which this conviction of the presence of God in

Jesus finally took in the Christian church. And it is faith in God's becoming man and his taking flesh in Jesus which also represents the real intention of the nativity story. Like that story, the creed says of the incarnation that Jesus was the Son of God from the beginning and is the Son of God in person. Yet the idea of incarnation stands in contradiction to the explanation which the tradition of Jesus' virgin birth originally meant to offer for his divine sonship and which formed the motive for the legend's development: if Jesus was God's Son in that he was created in Mary by God, then he could not be already God's son before, in the sense of pre-existence. The explanation of Jesus' divine sonship in the sense of his pre-existence and the explanation offered by the notion of his virgin birth contradict one another; and in this conflict we are bound to admit that the idea of pre-existence has greater material value. If Jesus did not only become the Son of God through the event of his resurrection; if the resurrection, rather, has the meaning of confirming his pre-Easter mission; and if this mission cannot be detached from Jesus' person, but is the justification for his divine authority – then the divine sonship of Jesus did not only begin with his baptism, the start of his public mission; it is the mark of his person from the very beginning. But if it is divine sonship in the sense of oneness with the being of God, it cannot be founded on Jesus' birth but must be thought of as participating in the eternity of God, as the idea of pre-existence expresses it.

In view of these facts, how can the contemporary Christian still go on repeating in church the phrase: 'conceived by the Holy Spirit, born of the Virgin Mary', as his own profession of faith? Does not everything we have said go to show that this sentence can no longer be a confession of faith on our part? Yet it is also clear that the Christian can very well assent to the intention which prompted the story of Jesus' virgin birth, even if this intention has grown beyond the expression it found in the nativity legend to the idea of the pre-existence of the sonship of Jesus in the eternal nature of God. Moreover the Christian today can also share the intention which allowed this formula to be absorbed into the creed. In the first place the point was to show that the Son of God is really identical with the historical person, Jesus of Nazareth. God does not only walk among men in human dress, a dress which can equally well be laid aside again at will. On the contrary, in Jesus Christ God has finally bound himself to this person and thus to mankind. This goes together with the second point, that Jesus did not only become Son of God at some particular point of time during his lifetime, but was, and is, in his person from the very beginning the only Son of God, mankind's mediator of the sovereignty of God.

Seen in this light, the formula of the virgin birth is an expression of the final nature of the revelation of God in Jesus, of God's bond with this man, and through him with mankind. Probably most Christians today would personally look for a different way of expressing this intention from the one offered by the story of the virgin birth. But that is not of decisive importance where we enter into the confession of faith of others. For that, it is enough to agree with the intention, even if the expression of that intention which we take over at the same time cannot be our own. This is what justifies us in adopting the creed as an expression of the faith of the church, not only today but from its very beginnings. For the alternative would be, not to alter this particular formulation alone, but the whole creed in general. But it is only in the classic form it has acquired that the creed is the sign of the unity of Christianity throughout history; and that is the reason for its irreplaceable function in the services of the church today.

Suffered under Pontius Pilate, was Crucified, Dead and Buried

It is noticeable how fully the Apostles' Creed preserves the sufferings of Jesus in all their detail. The mention of the Roman procurator Pontius Pilate points to the fact that the passion of Jesus took place entirely in the public eye, in the full light of what is reliably historical. Then the individual stages of the events are carefully listed: crucified, dead, buried. Here a particular stress lies on the fact that Jesus' crucifixion ended with his death and that this death was sealed by his burial. For it is the death of the Son of God himself (which the Gnostic opponents of the church disputed) which for Christians guarantees the over-coming of death. In the text of the creed it is only the care with which the death and burial of Jesus are mentioned, as well as the crucifixion, which suggests the interpretation of the death of Jesus. For the rest it is marked at this point by an astonishing sobriety. Only the sequence of events is expressly mentioned – none of the early Christian interpretations of the death of Jesus. The old idea (which may go back to Jesus himself: Luke 13.33 and 34f.) that Jesus had to suffer the fate of all prophets is missing. The creed contains not a word about the divine necessity for the death of Jesus in the light of Old Testament scriptural evidence. This idea was developed in the early Christian writings in a different direction. Thus we find the suffering and death of Jesus interpreted as expiation in the early church. The tradition of the Lord's Supper talks about the blood shed 'for many' (Mark 14.24) or 'for you' (Luke 22.20). In other passages we find the death of Jesus interpreted as a payment of the ransom for our sins (Mark 10.45), as an ex⁄ piatory sacrifice in the cultic sense (Rom. 3.25 and in the Epistle to the Hebrews), as the sacrifice which seals the completion of the new covenant of God with men. All these images, taken from the scriptural evidence of the Old Testament for the divine necessity of the death of Jesus, contain the idea that his sufferings were vicarious, borne in our stead. This idea, too, is only indirectly referred to in the Apostles' Creed, simply through the especial stress which is laid on Jesus' death and burial.

Anyone who wants to be clear about the sense in which the death of Jesus can take on a vicarious, or perhaps representative, significance ought to start from the question of the relation between the arrest and condemnation of Jesus, and the unique character of his message and activity. It seems unlikely that Jesus was actually seeking out death as the evangelists interpret it, especially through the prophecies of the passion, when he took his last journey to Jerusalem. The prophecies of the passion are, in the opinion of the vast majority of modern scholars, not the authentic words of Jesus himself. We must rather see them as the expression of the foreseeing of events which the later church ascribed to Jesus. We, on the contrary, have to hold fast to the character of these events as genuine, unforseeable experiences. They were not simply arranged by Jesus, though it is true that we can hardly avoid the assumption that Jesus must have reckoned with the clear possibility that his journey to Jerusalem might have a catastrophic end (Luke 13.32); for he had ex⁄ perienced the end of John the Baptist and shared the Jewish tradition of the sufferings of the prophets. But we can hardly look for the point of the journey in a deliberate self⁄sacrifice on the part of Jesus, planned from the beginning. The point must rather have been to force the Jews in the capital city to a decision for or against his message. Moreover, in what way ought a deliberately planned self-sacrifice on the part of Jesus to be interpreted? For what purpose was the sacrifice to be made? The idea that the death of Jesus was an expiation of the sins of the world must be seen as a retrospective interpretation of the event, rather than an effect deliberately brought about by Jesus.

Little is definitely known about the course of Jesus' trial. Jesus seems to have been brought under suspicion among the Romans of attempts at sedition. He was crucified as a rebel, as a Messianic pretender; so much is certain from the inscription on the cross. The suspicion of sedition was certainly slanderous, since Jesus not only laid no claim to the Messianic title but probably expressly rejected it. How could the accusation, there-fore, have been made? That the Jewish authorities played their part in it and that Jesus was cross-examined by the Jewish Sanhedrin before he was handed over to Pilate has occasionally been doubted, but probably without sufficient reason. If the Jewish authorities had not been involved, they could and would have defended Jesus against so mistaken a reproach. But what made them intervene, and why was Jesus then delivered over to the procurator's court under false accusation?

These questions are not easily answered. Perhaps the Jewish leaders were afraid that the stir which Jesus had made among the people might, if they did not intervene, bring them under suspicion of a seditious attitude themselves. But in addition a conflict already existed in any case between Jesus and the custodians of the Jewish tradition, for other reasons: the claim to authority which was expressed in Jesus' whole demeanour, the claim with which Jesus set himself above the authority of the Law, was bound to appear as positive blasphemy to those Jews who only judged his behaviour from the outside and who did not permit themselves to be captured by the passion of his message about the kingdom of God. The concept of blasphemy seems to have been so broad at that time that it covered every slur on the divine authority of the Law. And in this sense the 'But I say to you' which Jesus set over against the traditional words of the Law in the 'antitheses' of the Sermon on the Mount was bound to be understood as blasphemy, just as much as the saying against the continued existence of the temple, which may perhaps have sparked off the Sanhedrin's intervention. The fact that in spite of this the Jewish authorities none the less did not themselves order Jesus' execution through stoning, but handed him over to be condemned by the Romans under a false accusa⁄tion, may have been because the Romans had at that time reserved criminal justice for themselves – though this is doubtful; or it may simply be explained by the Jewish authorities' wish to avoid the indignation of Jesus' supporters.

At all events, the real, deeper reason for the trial, condem⁄nation and execution of Jesus must be looked for in the conflict with the Jewish authorities in which he was bound to be involved as a result of the whole nature of his behaviour – behaviour which is quite correctly described by the reproach of blasphemy. Thus far the representatives of the Jewish authorities did not act out of individually reprehensible intentions; when they repudiated Jesus and contributed to his condemnation, they were acting as the representatives of the Israelite tradition and the Jewish people. On the other hand, they did not in so doing necessarily act in the name of that people's true election and calling. Their right to speak and act for God's chosen people of Israel cannot remain untouched by the fact that the God of Israel himself, through the raising of Jesus, recognized the claim made by Jesus' proclamation of the imminent rule of God, a claim which might well appear as blasphemy to a traditionally⁄minded Jew in the ambiguity of the pre⁄Easter situation, because of Jesus' lack of respect for the Law.

The question of the extent to which the Jewish leaders of the time were involved in the trial of Jesus can hardly be discussed today without prejudice, after almost two thousand years of Christian enmity towards the Jews because of the deicide laid at the door of the whole Jewish people. The appalling history of Christian enmity towards the Jews was encouraged in the first place by an error; for the Gentile Christian church laid responsibility for the death of Jesus on the Jewish people alone, in contrast to the rest of mankind, instead of seeing the Jewish people as representatives of mankind in general, even in its participation in the trial of Jesus. By vindicating the non-Jewish section of mankind through the accusation of the Jewish people – in a highly un-Christian attitude of mind – the solidarity between Christians and God's chosen people, on which Paul still laid such stress, disintegrated. This renunciation of solidarity with the Jewish people because of the cross of Jesus was probably the decisive precondition for Christian enmity towards the Jews. It expressed itself in the non-biblical view that God had finally repudiated Israel because of the crucifixion of Jesus and had withdrawn Abraham's election from the Jews in order to transfer that election to the church, as the new Israel. This attitude, which was for so long a burden on the relationship between Christians and Jews, was revised in 1948 by the First General Assembly of the World Council of Churches in Amsterdam, with the admonition that in Christian instruction 'the events which led to the crucifixion should not be so depicted that they burden the Jewish people of today with a responsibility which belongs to mankind as a whole and not any *one* race or community'. In a similar sense the Second Vatican Council's declaration on the relation of the church to the Jewish people objected to the Jews being depicted as 'rejected or cursed by God'.

But what has to be corrected today is not only the renunciation of solidarity with the Jewish people because of the cross of

Jesus – which, after all, rather reconciled Jew and Gentile, according to Eph. 2.14–16. It is just as important for the present discussion between Christians and Jews that the Jewish people should not be identified as a whole and for all time with the actions of its leaders at that period. That is why the declaration of the Second Vatican Council runs: 'Although the Jewish leaders and their supporters urged the death of Jesus, the events of his passion can none the less not be laid at the door of all Jews living at that time without distinction, or at the door of Jews today.'

It is true that this sentence takes as its starting point the perspective of individual responsibility. It therefore frees particular individuals of the time, as well as later generations of the Jewish people, from responsibility for the death of Jesus. It does not, however, express an opinion on the question which is basic for the traditional view: namely, how far the Jewish authorities who were involved in Jesus' trial acted in the name of the Jewish people. But that is the decisive point. On the one hand the efficacy of the vicarious significance of Jesus' death, not only for his judges but for the whole Jewish people, and beyond them for mankind, depends – as we shall see in more detail later – on the question whether the Jewish authorities of the time were involved in Jesus' trial not only as individuals but also as official representatives of the Jewish people; and the same applies, accordingly, to the involvement of Pilate as representative of Rome and, beyond Rome, as the representative of state authority in general. On the other hand, however, in the light of Jesus' resurrection, not only is the justice of the verdict passed on him condemned; so also is the legitimation of his Jewish judges to pass judgment on him in the name of the chosen people. And by the same token the legitimation of Jesus' judges to pass final judgment on him in the name of the authentic heritage of Israel (and with it the tradition which was constitutive for the Jewish people) is also annulled, although this does not affect the representative significance of the death of Jesus for the Jewish people, and thus for mankind, as chosen by God. On the contrary, the election of the Jewish people is verified by the resurrection of Jesus, as the one united to the God who raised him from the dead (contrary to the verdict of his judges) and whom Jesus had earlier proclaimed as the God of the coming kingdom. Consequently, in the light of the Easter event, it becomes possible for the Jews particularly to revise the verdict once passed on Jesus, as being unjust and as not having been passed once and for all in legitimate representation of God's chosen people. Moreover, this possibility is open whether the revision takes place expressly on the grounds of the Christian Easter faith or whether it is drawn from a better understanding of the Jewish tradition. Here the possibility of a revision of the Jewish verdict on Jesus affects the understanding of the people of God themselves; it does not merely permit a special exception to be made for particular individuals.

The vicarious or representative meaning of the death of Jesus has been the premise of these reflections. That vicarious meaning rests on the fact that in the perspective of Easter everything that has gone before shows itself in a new and different light. God himself had now admitted Jesus' claim, which might earlier have seemed blasphemous to the Jew who was faithful to the Law, since it took up a position contrary to the authority of Moses. In the light of the resurrection of Jesus those involved seem to have changed places: now the people who condemned Jesus as a blasphemer stand there as blasphemers themselves, since Jesus has now been owned by God. This Jesus has, in the strict sense, died in their stead – for the crime of blasphemy, which his judges have themselves committed through their verdict. And through the very fact that these judges did not only act as isolated individuals but as the office-bearers of their people, the vicarious power of Jesus' death on the cross also extends beyond their sphere to the whole people, and indeed to the whole of mankind, since the Jewish nation, as God's chosen people, stands before God for the whole of mankind. It is these facts which must be seen as providing the essential basis for the Christian assertion of the vicarious efficacy of the death of Jesus.

The cross sheds a similar light on Pilate's involvement in the death of Jesus – and consequently the involvement both of Rome itself and the interest of political rule in general, which were embodied by Rome in the world of the day. The back-ground here is the conflict between Jesus' message and the claims of political rule. It is true that this conflict did not exist in the sense of the accusation made against Jesus, which imputed to him the intention of leading a national Jewish rising against the Roman occupying power. But Jesus' proclamation of the coming rule of God and its exclusive authority for men under-mined the spiritual foundations of the Roman *imperium* none the less. In the centuries that followed, this was rightly felt to be the case by the Roman emperors, to whom the Christians refused divine honours and sacrifice. The rule of God, understood in Jesus' exclusive sense, robs every political order of its absolute claim on the people living under it. The sharpness of this contrast was softened after Constantine by the view of imperial domination as the earthly reflection of the divine rule, a view which was indebted to the traditions of the ancient world. On the cross of Jesus, on the other hand, the contrast was evident in all its rigour. In the light of the divine proof of lordship in the resurrection of Jesus (although this feature was suppressed quite early on by the Christian tradition for apologetic reasons) the act of his condemnation appears as that very crime of lèse-majesté, the crime against the ruler, for which the Roman procurator had Jesus, the supposed or ostensible rebel, executed, though of course the majesty which is violated here is the majesty of God, no longer that of the Roman emperor. Thus the cross of Jesus demonstrates the tendency of political rule to violate the majesty of God, a tendency which operates everywhere where political rule usurps absolute binding force. At the same time it is clear in the light of the raising of the crucified Jesus that men are not bound in conscience to obey such claims, as the first Christians also showed later, through their resistance to the emperor cult. Through the raising of the one who was crucified, the individual is freed from the absolutely binding force of everything that counts in society. But political rule is not merely condemned, either. It is certainly humbled by the higher authority of God, who turned its judgment upside down by raising the crucified Jesus; but it is also pardoned on condition that it accepts this humiliation. For in this respect, too, we must speak of the vicarious or representative function of Jesus' death on the cross. The punishment for lèse-majesté which Jesus had to bear was inflicted on God by the statesman Pilate through his verdict on Jesus; that was shown when God put him in the wrong through the raising of Jesus. It is true that the substitution motif is connected here with the recognition of the God of Israel, who acted in Jesus' resurrection, as the only God of all men; and it acquires its relevance only in analogy to the substitution which is to be inferred through the light of his resurrection in Jesus' relationship to his Jewish judges. In this connection we must not already talk about substitution when another bears the punishment one has incurred oneself. This would only make matters worse, if one's own punishment were not thereby discharged and the guilt wiped out as well. The curious ex-change of positions between the righteous and the guilty in the trial of Jesus only has this vicarious meaning because, according to the message of Jesus, forgiveness of all sins is comprehended in trust in him as herald of the kingdom of God. That is why it is possible to say that for those who believe in him, his death was not only a bearing of the punishment for blasphemy; it also bore it away. On the great Day of Atonement in ancient Israel, the goat to which the High Priest was permitted to transfer the sins of the people, according to God's gracious decree, carried its guilt with it into the desert; and in the same way, as the church sings in the liturgy of the Lord's Supper, God has made Jesus the Lamb which has carried away the sins of the world.

Reflections of this kind presuppose that something like substitution or representation between men can exist, and that it is also possible in the sphere of human guilt especially. This has been continually disputed by critics of the church's doctrine of vicarious substitution, ever since the Socinians of the sixteenth and seventeenth centuries. People have protested especially in this connection against the possibility of substitution for moral guilt. It is true that another person can pay a debt of money for me; 'a moral debt, however, if it is not expiated by the one who has incurred it, is not expiated at all' (D. F. Strauss). Faustus Socinus thought that it would be unjust of God to punish the innocent for the guilty, especially because the guilty are, after all, in his power. This argument falls to the ground in the face of the ideas we have considered above, since the 'innocence' of Jesus as regards the reproach of blasphemy was only determined and demonstrated by his resurrection.

Moreover, the individualist concept of moral guilt, which is at the bottom of this criticism, is a dubious one. It is part of the social character of human existence for every individual con-stantly to incur responsibilities which more or less extend to others. Everyone is woven into the community in which he lives in his actions, and is involved in the actions of others. Thus in social life representation is a positively universal phenomenon. Even the structure of working life, with its division of labour, has the character of representation, which always includes an element of substitution. Anyone who does a job of work or practises a pro-fession is answerable in what he does for the whole which he serves, and he is equally dependent on the specific activities which others perform for his benefit. That the condition, for good or evil, of individuals or small groups can be borne vicariously for a whole community can be experienced in times of crises espec' ially. That was made particularly clear to the German people through the expulsion of the occupants of its eastern provinces and through the division of Germany, which meant that the different sections of the German people had to bear the conse' quences of the war to a varying degree. Much that happens to a community as a whole affects certain of its members, or a part of it, in a particular way; and in such a situation the part represents the whole society. The individualism of ethical responsibility can never entirely free itself from these involvements, without losing its connection with the reality of human life. On the other hand, however, we can only usefully enquire into the vicarious meaning of the death of Jesus under the premise of the general significance of substitution in man's social life. For with' out the general phenomenon of substitution in man's social life, the Christian doctrine of the vicarious efficacy of Jesus' death would remain a futile assertion.

The vicarious efficacy of the death of Jesus applied in the first place to God's chosen people Israel, as we saw above. But the very circumstance that Israel was chosen vicariously by God as repre' senting the whole of mankind and, further, the part played by Pilate in Jesus' crucifixion, showed that the death of Jesus has representa' tive significance, not only for Israel but for all men. The general validity of the meaning of Jesus' death for salvation is, indeed, dependent on the fact that all men participate in their lives in that opposition to God which is shown in Jesus' condemnation by his judges. That is why Paul was able to make the univer' sality of man's sin the condition of the cross's significance for the salvation of all men. Because all have sinned, because all live in the blasphemous state of existence which found expression in the rejection of Jesus as blasphemer by the very leaders of the people chosen by God himself: that is why Jesus bore the punishment for blasphemy, not for the Jewish people alone but for all men. The universality of sin makes possible the universality of salvation and redemption (Rom. 11.32; 3.21ff.). Thus the rejection of Jesus by his people has become through God's decree the reconciliation of the world (Rom. 11.15). For Paul this did not remain merely a general assertion; it became a historically effective force – one which changed the world. For the rejection of Jesus in the name of the Law had cancelled the Law itself, and so made possible the Pauline message of access to salvation through Jesus without the Law.

The vicarious efficacy of Jesus' death does not, of course, now mean that because Jesus has died for us, no one else has to die. It only means that from now on no one has to die alone any longer, because in death especially he has communion with the death of Jesus. This communion between our human dying and the dying of Jesus is the essential substance of the representative significance of Jesus' death. Because Jesus gathers up our dying into his own, the character of our dying changes. In communion with Jesus it loses its hopelessness and has already been overcome through the life which has appeared in Jesus' resurrection. The death of the blasphemer, the one who is shut out from all communion with God, has been taken away by Jesus once and for all. This separation from God – from the origin of all life – is after all the ultimate gravity of death, if we, like Paul, understand death as the seal of man's self-alienation from the divine origin of life. But since Jesus died, no one who lives and dies in communion with Jesus and in trust in him need die this death any more. In communion with Jesus' death, a death which was followed by the endorsement of Jesus by God himself, our dying loses its desolation and is turned into a dying in hope.

He Descended into Hell

The mention of Jesus' descent into hell is one of the latest components of the Apostles' Creed. In the baptismal creed of the church in Rome, which goes back to the second century, there was no mention of Christ's descent into hell. The reference to it between Jesus' burial and his resurrection was only inserted in the fourth century. The intention was no doubt to give a more detailed description of what happened to Jesus at his death: he did not only endure death in its physical aspect, but also experienced what death, as the fate brought about by sin, means for a man as person – namely, exclusion from God and his salvation.

We have already discussed this meaning of Jesus' death in connection with the events of his crucifixion and death. For Jesus died as one cast out, at least by the religious authorities of his people. That was bound to mean for him as a Jew that God himself rejected him – although on the other hand he knew himself to be sent and commissioned by God. Just because Jesus had proclaimed the nearness of God as no other had done, the rejection inflicted on him in the name of this same God was bound to affect him particularly profoundly.

It is true that death seals for all men that separation from God which is the real essence of the failure of existence to find its mark, the essence of sin, the essence of man's hardness of heart. Man cuts himself off from the origin of all life by relying on himself and shutting himself up within himself. Death makes this clear. But who of those who die really experiences it? Is it not the very triviality that so often characterizes the act of dying which is so especially shocking to the survivors who look on? Today, particularly, there seems to be hardly any preparation for death, such as was practised in the Christian Middle Ages. Most people turn their eyes away from the necessity of death as long as they possibly can. We hide our sick and dying behind the sterile walls of a hospital. And the sombre depths of human death are usually veiled even from the dying themselves by suffering or by the clouding of the consciousness. These sombre depths of human death are only realized where death is experienced as exclusion from God; and that can only be the case to the degree to which a person knows the nearness of God. To be fully conscious of the nearness of God and yet to be excluded from him is what the ancient dogmas saw as the tortures of hell. Luther's interpretation of Christ's descent into hell was therefore essentially correct when he saw it as the crucified Jesus' agony of conscience, the mental anguish which the proclaimer of the nearness of God must have experienced, knowing himself bound in conscience by that God to the authority of the Jewish tradition from which he had now been excluded.

The idea of hell in its individual features, as these have been delineated in so many pictures of the Judgment, is certainly fantastic. What these pictures have to say about the tortures of hell must be judged as pretty inadequate because the really decisive feature, the exclusion from communion with the living God, is not to be found in the traditional representations of the bottomless pit. Yet this fundamental feature of the idea of hell is the only one to which theology must hold fast and which it must free from the horrific fantasies of an imagination running riot. To be excluded from the nearness of God in spite of a clear knowledge of that nearness: that would be real hell. The question of the 'place' where hell is, therefore, derives from an inappropriate and for us superseded way of thinking. Neither heaven nor hell can be fitted into the time and place co-ordinates of the world of the modern experience of nature. But what is in question is not merely a pictorial description of the experience of conscience. Although Luther associated the crucified Jesus' agony of conscience with the tradition of his descent into hell, this does not mean that in our life the experience of conscience is the only reality which corresponds to the idea of hell. Since most people do not live their lives in that experience of the nearness of God which was characteristic of Jesus, they will not come up against the experience of hell either, since this presupposes knowledge of the nearness of God. But the fact that we cannot escape this experience by simply looking the other way is indicated by the idea of the judgment of the dead, to which we shall return at a later point.

It was part of the special destiny of Jesus already to have experienced in his conscience the reality of hell during his physical death. The connection between conscience and the experience of hell is not a phenomenon of human experience which is to be found everywhere in this way. It does not arise in normal human experience at all, but characterizes the particular kind of experience present in Jesus' death.

Now, in the history of theology a quite different interpretation of Jesus' descent into hell from all that we have suggested has been continually upheld. According to this, the descent into hell was not so much an expression of Jesus' sufferings as a demonstration of his triumph. The descent into hell is envisaged as a triumphal progress, and has often been so depicted in Christian art: in hell the risen Christ reduces the devil to submission and frees Adam and Eve, the first parents of the human race, from the bottomless pit. A similar view is already to be found in the New Testament, in the only passage in which Christ's descent into the realm of the dead is clearly mentioned, and with some detail. In the First Epistle of Peter we read that

Christ 'went and preached to the spirits in prison, who formerly
did not obey, when God's patience waited in the days of Noah'
(3.19f.). That these 'spirits' were the 'shades' of the disobedient
dead, as they are elsewhere in Jewish literature, is suggested by
a later phrase which occurs in the same epistle, where we read
(I Peter 4.6) that 'the gospel was preached even to the dead'.
The preaching of the gospel by Jesus even in the underworld
can doubtless only mean that he preached repentance. This then
means in its turn that those who are already dead are also still
reached by the Christian message. Salvation from future judgment is still made available in the realm of the dead to those who
during their lifetime encountered neither Jesus nor the Christian
message. Christian interpreters were already toning down the
full boldness of this idea even in the early period of the church.
We can read again and again that Jesus preached in Hades only
to the righteous men of ancient Israel, or only to men in general
who were righteous during their lifetime. But I Peter goes
further when it talks about the preaching of repentance. The
tendency towards a universalist understanding of salvation,
which is aimed at there, has found its full expression in the idea
that Christ also redeemed Adam – i.e. man *per se* – from the
underworld, an idea which we find in Origen and which generally stands in the forefront in paintings of Christ's descent into
hell.

How, then, does this interpretation of Jesus' descent into hell
relate to the first, which viewed it as the description of Jesus'
sufferings? The two ideas seem mutually exclusive. But they
have one thing in common. Both are interpretations of the death
of Jesus. And in this they belong together. For in that he died
forsaken by God, Jesus overcame death, as the state of being
forsaken by God, for all those who are united with him. The
vicarious significance of the death of Jesus finds expression in
the notion of his victory over hell. The cross has this victorious

meaning only in the light of his resurrection, which is the reason why the descent into hell was ascribed to the risen Jesus, although it has to do with the meaning of his cross. But of course the alternative of whether it was the crucified or the risen Lord who descended into hell (which was one of the points of controversy between Calvinist and Lutheran dogma) could only occur today to the kind of mind which confuses the image with the thing itself.

The idea in I Peter which describes Jesus' victory over hell as a preaching of repentance, takes the image of the early Christian missionary proclamation; and this notion brings out the universal scope of Jesus' act of representation or substitution in his cross and the universality of salvation mediated through it. It has often been asked: if God was revealed in Jesus for the first time, and if salvation for mankind only appeared in Jesus, what is to happen to the multitude who lived before Jesus' ministry? And what will become of the many who never came into contact with the Christian message? What, finally, is to happen to the people who have certainly heard the message of Christ but who – perhaps through the fault of those very Christians who have been charged with its proclamation – have never come face to face with its truth? Are all these people delivered over to damnation? Do they remain shut out for ever from the presence of God which has been made accessible to mankind through Jesus?

The Christian faith can say 'no' to this urgent question. That is the meaning of the phrase about Christ's descent into hell in the creed. We do not know whether it is the meaning intended by the men who included the formula in the creed. But it does in any event contain this meaning in the light of its New Testament origin: what took place for mankind in Jesus also applies to the people who either never came into contact with Jesus and the message about him, or who have never really caught sight of the truth of his person and his story. In a way that is hidden from us – and in a way hidden even from themselves – the lives of these people may yet be related to the revelation of God which appeared in Jesus. This must also apply, even without their knowing it, to the people about whom Jesus talked in the beatitudes – people who, quite independent of an encounter with Jesus, simply on the basis of their situation or their behaviour, have no other hope apart from the God whose nearness and whose coming kingdom Jesus preached. So even the people who never knew Jesus are, in a way which neither they nor we can understand, also related to Jesus and the God whom he preached through the great context of humanity and its history. And this relationship means for them, too, salvation or judgment. We have, it is true, no guarantee of their salvation. Salvation is only guaranteed to the man who has definite communion with Jesus – and who has through this communion the hope of overcoming death with Jesus. But all other men, too, even those who died before Jesus' ministry, can achieve the salvation which appeared in him – even if in ways which are beyond our comprehension. The meaning of the Christian acknowledgment of the conquest of the kingdom of death and Jesus Christ's descent into hell lies in the universal scope of salvation. Anyone who has grasped this can only regret that this particular article of the Apostles' Creed has recently come up against such special lack of understanding and has consequently frequently been rejected altogether.

The Third Day He Rose Again from the Dead, He Ascended into Heaven

The resurrection of Jesus is the event which was, historically speaking, the point of departure for the history of Christendom. In particular, the Easter event forms the starting point for the history of faith in Christ. And this starting point is at the same time the permanent, substantial foundation for that faith. Historical origin and substantial foundation are here one.

It is only possible to assert even that Jesus is Israel's promised Messiah, the Christ, in view of the confirmation of his mission through the raising of the one who was crucified. For it was through this, and through this alone, that Jesus, who was rejected by Israel, was shown to be God's only Son, and our Lord as well as Lord of the whole world. It is only in the light of the raising of Jesus that we have reason to speak of a divine incarnation in his person. The doctrine of the incarnation only develops in retrospect what the raising of Jesus means for the whole of his earthly activity and his person. And finally it is only in the light of the raising of Jesus that his death takes on the meaning of the vicariously accomplished reconciliation of mankind. If Jesus had not been raised from the dead, it would be impossible to ascribe any saving meaning to his death, for that death could then only have meant the failure of his mission and nothing else. The creed's further statements about Jesus

Christ are also in fact based on the Easter event: both the acknowledgment of Jesus' exaltation to the right hand of God, to participation in the divine power, as well as the expectation of his coming again to judgment, are to be understood as consequences arising from the fact of his resurrection from the dead.

In the resurrection of Jesus we therefore have to do with the sustaining foundation of the Christian faith. If this collapses, so does everything else which the Christian faith acknowledges. Of course this does not mean that the event of the raising of Jesus, taken as an isolated happening, would have this absolutely fundamental significance. It rather belongs originally within the same context as the life of Jesus which preceded it. It thereby gives this context a new foundation, and sets it in an entirely new light, by bringing the final endorsement of Jesus' earthly activity and his incomparable claim to authority in an unforeseen way, in the light of the last judgment, though not yet as the discontinuance of mankind's history through that divine judgment. The resurrection of Jesus is on the one hand, that is to say retrospectively, bound up with his earthly activity. On the other hand it points forward, being linked up with the eschato⁄ logical expectation of the judgment and the transformation of all things. This whole context only emerges in the way which is characteristic of the Christian faith in the light of the resurrection of Jesus; it stands and falls with that event.

Let us now turn to the question of what is actually meant by the assertion of this event. What is supposed to have happened, when we talk about Jesus' resurrection from the dead?

The most obvious thing, no doubt, would be to think first of the revival of a dead person: that is to say, of his return to life. But this idea is inapposite. The resurrection of Jesus was not a return to life as we know it; it was a transformation into an entirely new life. This distinction is of decisive importance for our understanding both of the early Christian Easter message and the Christian resurrection hope.

An indication of this is already given by the linguistic structure of the phrase 'to rise' or 'to be raised from the dead'. Linguistically this is a pictorial saying, a metaphor. What happens to the dead corresponds to the way in which a man is woken from sleep and gets up. The unheard-of and, in its actual reality, inconceivable happening which is expected as the future of the dead, is imagined pictorially, on the analogy of the every-day process of waking from sleep.

If we look carefully at the metaphorical structure of the idea of a resurrection from the dead, we can see that the idea of revival is by no means the only appropriate one. It is possible to talk quite unmetaphorically about the revival of a dead person. For this the pictorial language of the resurrection faith is not necessary. Metaphor is only unavoidable if we are dealing with a transformation into a reality which is entirely unknown to us – if we have to talk about it at all. For this reality is as such un-known to us; it quite obviously does not belong to the constantly recurring events of our everyday lives.

Paul made it unequivocally clear that for him 'resurrection from the dead' did not mean the return to earthly life, but a transformation into the new life of a new body. In I Cor. 15. 35–56 Paul expressly deals with the question how we ought to think of the physical reality of the person raised from the dead. Here it counts for him as being a settled thing that the future body will be a different body from the present one; it will not be a physical body but – as Paul expresses it – a 'spiritual body' (I Cor. 15.43f.). What he means by this is not a disembodied spirituality, in the sense of some Platonic tradition or other; in Paul's sense God's 'Spirit' is the creative origin of all life, and a spiritual body is a living being which, instead of being separated from this origin – as we are in our present existence – remains united with it; so that it is a life which no death can end any more. Paul describes the relation of the immortal, spiritual body to the present mortal, physical body as a radical transformation: 'I tell you this, brethren: flesh and blood cannot inherit the king, dom of God, nor does the perishable inherit the imperishable' (v.50). On the other hand, it is the present, mortal body which will experience this 'transformation': 'For this perishable nature must put on the imperishable, and this mortal nature must put on immortality.' The transformation of what is mortal into a spiritual body will therefore be on the one hand so radical that nothing remains unchanged. On the other hand, however, it is this present earthly body which will experience the transforma, tion; so that the transformation stands in a relationship to our present existence. What is to be created in place of the present body is not something totally different from it.

What Paul has to say here does not apply in the first place to the resurrection of Jesus especially; his subject is the resurrection which Christians have to expect. For Paul, however, the two belong together. In his view, the resurrection of Jesus justifies Christians in hoping for their own resurrection. It is of the greatest importance for him that Christians should participate in that particular reality which has already appeared in Christ. Paul cannot, therefore, have understood Jesus' resurrection as a mere revivification of his body either, but only as a radical transformation. This is particularly important, since in the First Epistle to the Corinthians we have the only extant account of Jesus' resurrection which derives from a man who had himself seen the risen Lord. All the other New Testament accounts of the appearances of the risen Jesus had passed through many hands before they acquired the form in which we have them. It is only with Paul and his remarks about the reality of the resur, rection that we have to do with an eye,witness's own words. The appearance of Christ which Paul experienced must, however, in view of all that we have discussed, have been of such a kind that it could not be confused with that of a revivified corpse. Otherwise Paul would not have been able to talk as he did about the resurrection reality as a transformation. He must have encountered a reality totally different in kind from all earthly life.

We must therefore conclude that the resurrection from the dead of the Easter faith, which Christians also hope for in the future, must be sharply distinguished, not only from the raising of the dead which is also occasionally reported in the ancient world's accounts of miracle workers, but also from the raisings of the dead which the evangelists describe Jesus himself as performing – in the case of the young man of Nain, for example (Luke 7), or Lazarus (John 11). Quite apart from the question of the credibility of such more or less late and legendary accounts, the event which these stories have in mind is definitely quite different from what the witnesses of the resurrection of Jesus mean, or from what is meant by the early Christian hope. In the case of Lazarus and the young man of Nain, at the peak of the miraculous healing attributed to Jesus, it was only a temporary return to this life by someone already dead. There is no doubt whatever that the evangelists themselves believed that the people who were called back to life in this way none the less died again later. Their temporary revival is only a sign of the reality which has already appeared in Jesus' resurrection and towards which the Christian's future hope is directed. Here what is in question is life of a quite different kind, an immortal life no longer bounded by any death, which must therefore be in any case totally different from the form of life of organisms known to us.

If we go on to ask where Paul acquired his conception of the mode of the resurrection life, it is not sufficient to point to the appearance of the risen Jesus which was bestowed on him; we must note that Paul already belonged to an older, Jewish tradition, in which the expectation of the resurrection of the dead had already been developed – whether it be the resurrection of all men or only of the righteous. This expectation found its expression above all in what are known as the apocalyptic writings, which came into being in the Judaism of the Persian period, after the return from the Babylonian exile, and especially in the last two centuries before Christ. Examples of the beginnings of this literature can still be found in the Old Testament canon in Isaiah 24–26 and in the Book of Daniel. Other writings, some of them almost as old, were no longer received into the Old Testament canon – for example the Ethiopic Book of Enoch, which in its turn consists of a collection of different apocalyptic works. The interpretation and classification of this literature is still hotly disputed today; but some of its ideas were also shared by the Pharisaic movement at the time of Jesus. And this applies particularly to the expectation of the resurrection of the dead.

The apocalyptic expectation of a future resurrection of the dead – combined with the idea of a final divine judgment – may perhaps have been influenced by related Persian ideas. But the expectation of the resurrection was not a foreign colouring which the Jewish faith acquired from outside influences. It must, rather, be seen as the answer to a question which arose in the Jewish tradition itself, namely, how the righteousness of God was to be fulfilled in the individual. For the righteousness of God is demonstrated in the correspondence between what one does and what happens to one, in the life of man; but this does not work out in the life of the individual. Consequently, if the correspondence is to be implemented for every individual, there must be compensation in a life beyond the grave. The resurrection of the dead was not, however, already understood everywhere as being the reality of salvation, as it was in Paul; it was generally seen as the gateway opening to glorification for the one, and judgment and eternal punishment for the other. In this connection the expectation of resurrection was apparently linked quite early on with the idea of a transformation, and especially with the transformation of the raised righteous to greater glory, such as is possessed by the angels or the stars of heaven. More detailed reflections about the process of transformation itself, such as we find in Paul in I Cor. 15, can only be found for the first time in the apocalyptic writings of the first century AD, that is to say, among Paul's contemporaries.

Jesus himself seems incidentally to have shared the notion of a transformation in connection with the resurrection. According to Mark 12.25, when the Sadducees (who did not believe in the resurrection) asked Jesus about the life of those who had been raised, he answered that they neither marry nor are given in marriage but are like angels in heaven. Luke 20.36 adds: 'for they cannot die any more.' At all events, the intention of the entirely traditional reference 'to be like angels' suggests that it is, for earthly beings, an entirely new kind of existence, similar to what Paul has in mind when he talks about the 'spiritual body'. Both Jesus and Paul therefore belonged to a particular tradition of Jewish theology in their ideas about the form of life enjoyed by those who have been raised from the dead.

The development of the hope of a resurrection from the dead, as expressed in the apocalyptic writings, first gave Paul the opportunity of describing the particular event which he ex⁄perienced, like other disciples of Jesus before him, as a reality similar in kind to the life of the resurrection. Paul therefore called the possibility of a general resurrection of the dead the presupposition for acknowledgment of the resurrection of Jesus: 'If the dead are not raised, then Christ is not raised' (I Cor. 15.16). On the other hand the event of the raising of Jesus also has a retrospective effect on the expectation of a resurrection of the dead in general. It not only strengthened this expectation, it was a guarantee to those united with Jesus that they, too, would in the future participate in the life which had already appeared in him.

It was along these lines that Paul developed his ideas of a specifically Christian resurrection hope after his remarks in the First Epistle to the Thessalonians about the participation in salvation of those Christians who had died while waiting for the delayed second coming of Christ, which had originally been expected to take place in the immediate future (I Thess. 4. 13ff.). The Jewish expectation of the resurrection, in so far as it was hope for the resurrection of all men, had not been a specific expectation of salvation: it was to open up the way to salvation for the one, and to judgment for the other. But in so far as the resurrection counted as being already the reality of salvation itself, it was not promised to everyone, but merely to the righteous. In any case, the question of who was to partake in the salvation of a new life with God remained open. Whereas Jewish tradition answered this question with: through observance of the Law, for Christians Jesus was the criterion of participation in salvation. The resurrection of Jesus assured those who are united to him through faith that they too will participate in the life which has already appeared in him. Here, therefore, as is clearly evident in Paul, the expectation of the resurrection is itself already the hope of salvation. Although in this way the specifically Christian hope of resurrection is founded on communion with the crucified and raised Lord, it none the less, like the Jewish tradition, presupposes the truth of the expectation of a general resurrection. This presupposition also underlies the message of the resurrection of Jesus.

If the credibility of the message of Jesus' resurrection therefore hangs together with the general question of whether a resurrection of the dead can be reckoned with in general, the same may be said of our contemporary historical judgment of the

Christian Easter tradition. If one starts from the premise that the dead remain dead, that death is the absolute end, and that nothing like a resurrection from the dead (in whatever sense one likes to take it) can ever happen, in any circumstances whatever, this produces so strong a prejudice against the Christian message of the raising of Jesus that one no longer weighs up in detail the exact quality of the evidence with regard to its significance for a total judgment, in the way that is, after all, otherwise the his-torian's duty and chief business. The possibility of an event such as is reported in the Christian message of Easter can only be seriously considered if the general expectation of a future resurrection of all men (or at least the righteous) from the dead is meaningful in itself, and if it is conceivable in the context of a contemporary understanding of reality.

The question of the raising of Jesus, as a question which is to be taken seriously historically speaking, can only be framed at all on the basis of a view of possibility which is not closed from the outset in this direction. Is the idea of a resurrection of the dead merely an alien substance in the context of what we know today about the elements of man's reality and the conditions of his self-understanding? Or does it stand in a significant relation to the constitutive conditions of man's situation? In view of today's anthropological insights particularly, strongly character-ized as they are by the viewpoint of the physical nature of human existence, the idea of a resurrection of the dead could be more seriously judged than in earlier periods, as being a motif of human self-understanding appropriate to the human situation. True, it is only possible to recognize and maintain the positive relevance of the idea of a resurrection of the dead in this way on condition that we are also clear about its pictorial and meta-phorical character. For anyone who views the idea of the resur-rection of the dead as a kind of supernatural knowledge of man's future concealed from all human experience, it is bound to remain an alien element in the context of human experience. It is only in its particular character as metaphor that it can be grasped as the expression of the situation of man in his self-understanding. For we still most readily become aware of the ultimate questions of our existence in the form of pictures and metaphors, and it is by no means a matter of indifference which pictures we take in our attempts to express the meaning, or meaninglessness, of our lives. Moreover, the use of biblical language does not mean that the speaker is not concerned with reality in what he says. But he is concerned with a reality which, because of its nature, can still best find a name through biblical language.

One of the things which distinguishes man from all other animals is that he is aware of the inescapability of his own death. It is an equally essential part of man to enquire beyond the limitations of his existence as to the fulfilment of his human destiny, which is only achieved in the individual life to a fragmentary degree at most. Knowledge of the limitations provokes the crossing of them, and indeed knowledge of the limitations is not possible without awareness of something beyond. It is true that the crossing of the frontiers of death, which has always taken place in the imagination, can be withdrawn through the verdict that there is nothing to be achieved in this direction except enthusiasm without purpose or justification. But without the question of fulfilment beyond the grave, life on this side of death would be meaningless, too. Conversely, in the light of a hope beyond death, our earthly life presents itself as the fragment of a greater whole, still veiled in mystery. It is true that we do not know what awaits us beyond death, in a dimension of reality hidden from our present experience. And yet men have continually tried to arrive at some idea of it, in order to assure themselves of their human destiny, which can find no completion in the limitations of this present life.

We can only form an idea of what is completely hidden from us on the analogy of what we know. This can take place in different ways. In our cultural tradition, the Greek belief in immortality and the biblical hope of the resurrection stand in contrast to one another here, as competing forms of expression of the same basic human experience, although they have also been combined in the history of Christian eschatology. As against the idea of the immortality of the soul, which right up to the nineteenth century actually counted as being demonstrable by reason, the biblical idea of a resurrection of the dead can today appear at once soberer and more appropriate. Soberer because in its confinement to the metaphor of waking up from sleep it remains mindful of the gap between this life and everything which lies beyond the frontiers of death – a gap which defies every claim to direct knowledge. The doctrine of immortality affirmed such knowledge, but was only able to support its claim by the illusion that the experience of the soul could be independ-ent of its physical conditions. The idea of a resurrection from the dead is at this particular point more in accord with our con-temporary knowledge of man, because in the imagery of its language it preserves the unity of the physical and the spiritual, without which we can no longer conceive human life. The idea of a resurrection of the dead is therefore especially appropriate as an expression of the question of man's destiny beyond death, which is essential to a clear self-understanding of human ex-istence in the face of death. The inescapability of this question for everyone who faces up to the relevance of his own death for his self-understanding, offers no guarantee of the reality of a life which overcomes death. But it keeps the mind alive to the idea that the secret of life surpasses all our present knowledge.

It is only on the basis of such a general attitude to the reality of life that we can usefully ask the question about the raising of Jesus in historical form at all. For it is only then that the question itself is not already distorted by prejudice. We then have to enquire whether the happenings which for the apostles of the early church became the origin of their mission, allow of a better interpretation for our historical understanding than is given by the pictorial language of the expectation of the resurrection, with which primitive Christianity described them; or whether this very picture language is the right form of expression for the reality to which these happenings refer us back.

It is essential to be clear about the inescapability and the essential possibility of the historical question as regards the resurrection of Jesus. It is inescapable for the historian if he wants to understand the history of Christianity's origins. But for the Christian, too, it is impossible to avoid forming a historical judgment about Jesus' resurrection, because we cannot directly see the present reality of the risen Jesus, but can only believe in it; again, we can only believe on the basis of the witness of the primitive church, which must in its turn be examined as to its credibility.

The fact that we have no direct experience of the reality of the risen Lord is implied by the story of Jesus' ascension in Luke: after the time of his appearances to the apostles, the risen Lord was snatched away from his church until the time of his second coming. The earlier primitive Christian tradition saw Easter and the Ascension as being closer together: the resurrection of Jesus as such coincided for the earliest witnesses with his being caught up 'into heaven', into the hidden realm of God. But in the main the earlier witnesses, Paul especially, are of the same opinion as Luke: the series of the constitutive appearances of the risen Jesus is finished – finished for Paul with the appearance to him himself. Jesus will only come again at the dawn of the end-time. In the intervening period there are no direct encounters with the one who is risen; there is only the word of his apostles. These witness that Jesus did not remain among the dead but was raised. If this witness can be believed, then we can of course also be certain that he lives and acts in the present as well; and that the reality of his resurrection, which continues even in the present, is efficacious especially through the preaching of that resur‐ rection as an event in the past. But such a conviction can un‐ questionably only be based on the information that Jesus did not at that time remain among the dead. Without this inform‐ ation, all present assurances from the pulpit that Jesus lives would remain emotional exaggeration and empty talk. The conviction that Jesus lives, even today, as the one who is risen, depends on the reliability of this information.

But how is it possible to form a judgment as to the reliability of the information that Jesus did not remain among the dead, but that he appeared in living form to his disciples shortly after his death and burial? Now, this information points to particular events which are supposed to have taken place at a particular time* – appearances of the Jesus who had previously died and been buried, and the finding of his empty tomb. The exam‐ ination of such assertions, however, can be carried out solely and exclusively by the methods of historical research. There is no other way of testing assertions about happenings which are

* The creed talks about Jesus rising again 'on the third day'. This dating goes back to Paul, who in I Cor. 15.4 passes on the information that Jesus was raised 'on the third day in accordance with the scriptures' (cf. also Acts 10.40). The reference to scripture has continually led to the supposition that the dating of the resurrection of Jesus which has been passed down to us is connected with a particular Old Testament passage, most probably Hos. 6.3: 'After two days he will revive us; on the third day he will raise us up, that we may live before him.' This saying was also interpreted by the Jews as referring to the resurrection of the dead in the end‐time, which makes an application to the Christian Easter tradition the more plausible. The influence of the early Christian scriptural proof on the tradition of Jesus' resurrection 'on the third day' does not, however, necessarily exclude the possibility that there was some historical occasion in the Easter experiences of the first Christians which could be read in the perspective 'of the Scriptures'. The point when Jesus' empty tomb was discovered has been thought of in particular.

supposed to have once taken place in the past. After all, the methods of historical research have been developed precisely for the examination of assertions of this kind, and every approach which is of use in such an examination would therefore *ipso facto* be proved part of the equipment of historical research.

One cannot, of course, make it too clear that in every his⁄torical judgment the evaluator's whole experience of the world and himself plays a part. Its influence will be all the greater, the more unusual the event is which is asserted by others and which now has to be evaluated. What this or that historian believes to be in any way possible depends on his own picture of reality and on the way in which he absorbs into this picture the points of view contributed by the various sciences, from physics to anthro⁄pology and sociology. The historian's judgment in a particular case is often determined and limited from the outset by his previous understanding as to the orbit of possibility. This is particularly clear in such an unusual problem as the question of Jesus' resurrection. Even for the primitive church this was not, after all, an everyday event. At first it was probably viewed as the beginning of the end, as the dawn of the eschatological reality of the divine rule, which would now soon be extended to all men. But as time passed and nothing more happened, the early church came to understand that the resurrection of Jesus was, for the present, a unique break⁄in of the reality of the end⁄time; and this experience profoundly altered the horizon of the apocalyptic expectation of the end.

Can, now, the historical mind suppose that the assertion of facts of this kind represents reality? Can the historian reckon with the break⁄in of an end⁄time reality which does not take the same form as other historical events and which rests on a radical transformation of the present world? Can he consider it possible for such an end⁄time reality to make itself felt beforehand, and already to become fully active in this present world?

Why should the historian not in fact be able to reckon with something like this in his critical investigation of the past? If the ideas of an end to all things and a resurrection of the dead can be otherwise justified as meaningful, why should they not be capable of finding a place in the historian's knowledge of reality, just as much as the facts of physics, biology, sociology and psychology? And why should he not then be able to weigh up the possibility that this end⁄time reality may make itself felt in advance, even if we can only talk about it in metaphors and even though it still remains a mystery in its unique character? Who is to say that the only things that can happen are the things which are by nature already fully and completely comprehen⁄ sible? Is not even our everyday reality more complex than a picture of reality so empty of mystery would like to admit?

One often hears the objection that a historian who reckoned with possibilities of this kind would come into conflict with the natural sciences. Curiously enough this objection is seldom raised by scientists nowadays, and least of all by physicists; it is most often heard on the lips of theologians, or even historians. In these quarters a dogmatic view of the natural sciences is evidently still widespread which is no longer held by the sciences themselves.

The natural sciences try to establish and describe laws from data. They do not decree what may be viewed as a datum in general, and what may not. At most they allow conclusions as to the events with which we can or must reckon. Science by no means determines the horizons of the future. And even in look⁄ ing at the past, conclusions can certainly be drawn about the prehistory of the earth and the universe, from natural laws which are known to us at the present day; and such conclusions must be confirmed or refuted by means of appropriate empirical clues. But on the other hand the same method by no means allows us to establish without more ado the possibility or impossibility of a single event which is otherwise vouched for. If it stands in contradiction to otherwise well-founded assumptions, these will at most make us suspicious of its credibility; but the suspicion can only be settled by a historical investigation of the assertion which has been passed down to us. The only thing which has to be excluded is the possibility of individual events being interpreted as the violation of otherwise valid natural laws; for that would eliminate the concept, or general applicability, of natural law itself. On the other hand, it is completely conceivable that without infringing the validity of the known natural law, but through the addition of unknown factors in a particular case, an event which seems to us unusual does genuinely exist. It is true that we can reckon with this in inverse proportion to the degree to which an alleged event resembles otherwise common occurrences. Thus the revival of a corpse, for example, once a very brief period of time has been exceeded, is bound to count as extremely improbable. In the case of the resurrection of Jesus, however, there are not even indications which might suggest such a judgment, for the happening which is asserted here is one whose final point lies in a sphere which is otherwise totally inaccessible to human experience and which can consequently only be expressed metaphorically or in other forms of a language which cannot yet be completely realized and controlled in empirical terms.

The natural sciences cannot, therefore, be the final court of appeal in the decision as to the possibility or impossibility of Jesus' resurrection. Such an appeal to science is a short circuit which continually obtrudes itself because the understanding of reality prevailing today is essentially determined by the world-picture of classical physics and especially by its view of nature's obedience to law. It is true that science itself is conscious that its formulae do not provide an exhaustive description of the reality of nature, but only describe it under a certain aspect – the aspect of natural law. But there is no picture of reality today which also takes account of the thus neglected aspect of the contingency of events, which is capable of associating that contingency with natural law, with the historicity of life, man and science itself, and which could in addition lay claim to a general applicability even approaching that of the natural sciences. Consequently it is understandable that there is an inclination to take generalized (and thereby simplified) scientific results dogmatically as the fundamental description of reality, and to go on from there to build up ideas about the uniformity of all happening which allow no room for the very unusual, let alone the exceptional. Yet it is possible to avoid such snap judg‑ ments, and for thinking people it is imperative to do so.

For the historian, this means that in forming a judgment about the past he must not from the outset permit only those possibilities which are in line with the normal and superficial course of events. He must never, of course, accept transmitted material without examination either. On the contrary, a con‑ siderable dash of scepticism is entirely appropriate to begin with when dealing with stories about the dead who come back to life. For such assertions are not unique in the literature of the ancient world. We meet them outside the biblical writings as well, even if they are not conceived in the same way. In many cases reports of this sort obviously bear the stamp of the legend‑ ary. The early Christian traditions must therefore be examined, in order to discover whether they show traces of legendary origin, or at least legendary accretions. Moreover we must enquire whether any traces are to be found in the accounts which point to the possibility that the appearances of the risen Jesus were hallucinations, in the strict psychiatric sense of the term. All such questions must be conscientiously considered. But the historian must also keep an open mind, in considering that many things happen which are not fully explicable according to the rules of normal events known to us. In particular, the person who is conscious that the question of the true reality of human existence can, for the time being, only find its answer in eschatological images, will consider the possibility that this reality might also make itself apparent in the events which he is investigating.

Such an investigation of the different New Testament tradi-tions about the resurrection of Jesus cannot be made here. But a brief summing up of the present state of research can be given: the traditions about the resurrection of Jesus do undoubtedly contain legendary elements. But it is impossible to prove that what is at issue is legend as a whole. On the contrary, the state of the traditions speaks against such an assumption, especially as regards the accounts of the appearances, but also in the tradition of Jesus' empty tomb, although in the latter case opinions are divided. Moreover, all attempts to explain the appearance of the risen Jesus as hallucinations have failed up to now. The neces-sary indications are lacking, or at least insufficient.

In view of this state of affairs, it is, of course, possible to suspend judgment altogether about the kind of events which may lie behind the traditions of Jesus' resurrection. But this means renouncing the possibility of understanding the origins of Christianity. If we ask about the origins of Christianity, not merely in the sense of enquiring what the first Christians believed, but in the sense of a present-day evaluation of what was really at the bottom of the story which started Christianity off, then we have to face up to the problem of the Easter events. Moreover it is perfectly possible to arrive at the opinion that, when one has subjected the early Christian traditions of Jesus' resurrection to a critical examination, the description of the event in the lan-guage of the eschatological hope still proves itself to be the most plausible, in the face of all rival explanations. Nobody could call this opinion indisputable. The matter is not historically decided, or decidable, in the sense that all further discussion about it is superfluous. But even after a careful examination of early Christian traditions, the assertion that Jesus is risen can be justified. As we have already said, a statement of this kind always also implies a historical claim, because it is the assertion of a particular past event; and with such an assertion it lays itself open to historical enquiry and examination. It can also be termed a historical statement, however, in the sense that it can be maintained in the face of an examination of this kind. This does not, it is true, mean a final and incontrovertible decision as to the facts. But that is not always possible in other historical judgments, either. In spite of that, the assertion that Jesus is risen from the dead remains a matter of dispute in a special degree because it cuts so deeply into fundamental questions of the understanding of reality.

The permanently controversial character of Jesus' resurrection need not disturb the Christian, however. He should not even find it surprising. For ought we to expect anything else, when it is only the ultimate divine future which will allow the new life that has appeared in Jesus to emerge as the general reality of God's new humanity? That general context of experience into which Jesus' resurrection can be fitted (in the sense of conforming to the rest of human reality) will only be established through the eschatological consummation of all things. Consequently Christianity will have to get used to the fact that the basic assertion of its faith will remain a matter of dispute in this world. But it is neither confuted, nor does it lack for evidence. If no arguments could be marshalled in its favour which would allow it to seem credible, then the assertion that Jesus is risen would be the expression of irresponsible subjectivism or blind faith in authority. But the cause of Christian faith does not rest on such shaky ground. On the contrary, the historical claim, which is already contained in the assertion that Jesus is risen, is a tenable one on objective examination, even in the context of our present experience of reality. The distance of the present world from the eschatological future of God does not exclude the real appearance of that future in our present world. And it is on this that the Christian faith has always insisted throughout history.

He Sits at the Right Hand of God the Father Almighty, From thence He Shall Come to Judge the Quick and the Dead

Here again we shall take two statements from the creed together in our discussion because of their close connection with one another. This was the case before, with Jesus' resurrection and ascension. But the reason here is different. With the resurrection of Jesus and his exaltation to God (or ascension) it became apparent that the two statements were originally based on one and the same event, since the resurrection of Jesus was originally thought of itself as an exaltation to God from the grave. Hence the appearances of the risen Jesus were experienced as happen‚ ings sent from heaven. The temporal distinction between resur‚ rection and ascension only seems to have come into being in a fairly late phase of the early Christian tradition, namely in the theology of Luke, towards the end of the first century. Moreover, it resulted from the more pronounced stress on the quasi‚earthly corporeality of the appearances of the risen Jesus: by this time these counted as meetings taking place on earth. But if the Easter appearances were understood as earthly encounters, then the carrying away of Jesus from earth had to be viewed as an additional, special event; and this is the way in which the story of Jesus' ascension is presented.

In the relationship between the sitting at the right hand of God and the coming again to judgment, we are not dealing with two associated aspects of one event, as in the case of Jesus' resurrection and ascension. Here we have to do with the cosmic function of the risen Jesus, that is to say with a further development of the meaning of the Easter event for the person of Jesus in its relation to the world. In this connection the two statements about the coming again to judgment and the sitting on the right hand of God follow one another, in a sequence. The coming again to judgment of the one who is risen is the basic statement, whereas the acknowledgment that Jesus now, already, rules over creation at the side of God is a conclusion drawn from this. The relationship between the substance of the two statements, and their relationship in the history of the tradition, does not therefore accord with their order in the text of the Apostles' Creed. There they are simply listed in the (supposed) temporal order of the events reported: the list of events in the earthly life and death of Jesus is followed by the statements about his present life and about his future. We already saw earlier that the Apostles' Creed would have to be differently ordered in some cases if the statements which are fundamental in substance and in the history of the tradition were put first and those which later developed out of them, in the course of the early Christian history of the tradition, were mentioned later. This would mean that the acknowledgment of Jesus' resurrection would have to stand right at the beginning, even before the mention of his dignity as Christ; and the statement about his second coming would have to follow, in a direct link with his resurrection; the title of Christ and Christ's present lordship at the side of God would only have to be mentioned after that; then the statements about his preexistence (as the onlybegotten Son) and his incarnation; and finally would come the mention of his vicarious sufferings. The acknowledgment of the second coming of Christ is therefore closely connected in essence with his resurrection, the two together forming the basis for all further theological statements about Jesus.

How did the expectation of Christ's second coming develop?

The idea of a divine judge who will descend from heaven to judge all mankind at the end of the world has its origin in pre-Christian times. Behind it lies the idea of a judgment of the dead, a notion which can be found in many religions, even apart from the idea of an end of the world. The association of the judgment of the dead with expectations of the end-time is to be found in Judaism, but also in Persian religion. In Judaism the Son of man is the judge of the end-time. The term Son of man can be already found in the Book of Ezekiel, as God's form of address to the prophet (e.g. Ezekiel 2.1ff.). There it simply means man – man as a single individual. By addressing the prophet in this way, God turns to him, not in the singularity of his personal existence, nor even as the holder of an office, nor as a member of his people, but as a creature: 'You individual man.' When Daniel in a night vision sees someone 'like a son of man' coming with the clouds of heaven (7.13), this is a symbol for the human character of the kingdom of God at the end of history, just as the beast figures mentioned earlier symbolize the succeeding world empires. In the Apocalypse of Enoch, however, this 'man' or Son of man who brings the divine kingdom of the end-time is thought of as a concrete individual figure, whose most important function is to be the judgment of the end-time. The 'man' or Son of man is now the judge of the end-time, who descends from God in the clouds of heaven; and this figure of Jewish expectation was identified with Jesus by the primitive Christian church in their expectation of Jesus' coming again to judgment. How did this merging of Jesus with the figure of the future judge of the world, the Son of man, come about? Can we discover anything about the motives which led to it?

Like John the Baptist before him, Jesus himself very probably talked about the future judgment of the Son of man. The sayings of Jesus about the Son of man which the evangelists have passed down to us fall into various groups, among which some, at least, of the sayings which point to the Son of man as future judge of the world are probably authentic. For in some of these sayings Jesus distinguishes the Son of man from himself, as a different person: 'Everyone who acknowledges me before men, the Son of man also will acknowledge before the angels of God' (Luke 12.8; cf. also 9.26 and Mark 8.38). The post-Easter church would have formulated these sayings differently; for it made Jesus one with the coming Son of man. This is also shown, accordingly, by Matthew's version of the saying just quoted 'Every one who acknowledges me before men, I also will acknowledge before my Father who is in heaven' (10.32). Unlike the version of the saying in Luke, here the 'I' of Jesus stands in both parts of the sentence. This is an expression of the primitive church's identification of Jesus with the Son of man. The historical Jesus, on the other hand, would probably have distinguished the Son of man from himself when he spoke of him, while proclaiming that his own message and behaviour would be confirmed through the coming judgment of the Son of man.

After Easter the distinction between the earthly person Jesus and the future world judge coming from heaven disappeared: through his resurrection Jesus had himself become a heavenly figure, just like the Son of man of Jewish ideas. The Christian future hope was now directed towards the coming again of the risen Lord to fulfil the rule of God which he had proclaimed. At the same time, the function of the risen Jesus automatically merged

to such a degree with the function of the Son of man who was ex⁄
pected to come to final judgment, that the church was now able
to recognize Jesus himself as the expected Son of man. Perhaps
some of his disciples already saw Jesus in the Easter appearances
simply as the Son of man: for the appearances are to be thought
of as incidents sent from heaven. At all events the appearance of
Jesus from heaven was probably so closely related to the picture
of the Son of man who was to come in the clouds of heaven that
the two could hardly continue to be distinguished, especially
since the world judgment could not be separated from the final
setting up of the rule of God. Jesus himself had linked his
message with the figure of the Son of man, from whose judgment
he expected its endorsement. After Easter it was no longer
merely the future function of the Son of man which was thought
of as corresponding to Jesus' earthly activity; the two figures
themselves now became identical.

Does all this still concern us today? The figure of the Son of
man became a colourless one quite early on in the Christian
tradition. True, in the Gentile church the coming again of
Jesus was still bound up with the judgment of the world, but
there ceased to be any mention of the Son of man. On the other
hand Jesus was talked about as being the new, second man, who
overcomes the sins of the first and brings man's destiny to fulfil⁄
ment. We already find this in Paul (Rom. 5; I Cor. 15). Here
the revelation of the new man was certainly still connected with
Jesus' resurrection, but no longer with the judgment of the world,
as was the case with the Jewish figure of the Son of man. Now,
the idea that the figure of Jesus – his teaching, his sufferings and
the overcoming of death through him – is the realization of the
humanity of man, or man's destiny as man, is basic to every
Christian faith today as well. It is also part of this conviction,
however, that Jesus provides the standard for the degree in
which we ourselves and all other men arrive at true manhood in

our lives. No one escapes this standard, whether he is a Christian or not. That means the expectation of Christ's second coming to judgment, an expectation directed towards a future which crosses the frontiers of our present life because the course of this world is marked by the prosperity of the godless, by the rule of conditions and modes of behaviour which are a mockery of man's humanity, and by the suffering of the innocent. Over against this the expectation of Christ's coming again to judgment is the foundation of that certainty of the standard by which the Christian withstands the pressure of ruling circumstances and the tendencies of the spirit of any given age.

The basic ground of this certainty is still the Easter event, even today. After Jesus' mission seemed to have collapsed with his crucifixion and his supporters were scattered, God acknow-ledged him through the resurrection and confirmed the claim of his message – the claim that the salvation of men, or their ruin, depends solely on their attitude towards the divine future and therefore also on their attitude to Jesus. The ultimate character of this claim of Jesus was authenticated through the appearance in himself of the final reality of the new man, of the resurrection of the dead. This already provides the reason why Jesus is the ultimate standard, the judge of the world who exercises judgment with the authority of God. Anyone who rejects Jesus and his message is judged by Jesus' own word: 'The word that I have spoken will be his judge on the last day' (John 12.48).

Because the future judge of the world is now one with Jesus, his judgment is no longer reserved for the future alone. In a secret way it is already exercised in the present. But it will only become manifest with the full dawn of the kingdom of God, with the resurrection of the dead and the renewal of creation. The judgment of the world which is associated with the final coming of God's kingdom will bring the unveiling of every-thing which is already secretly determined. Christians also move towards this judgment, and in the light of the consummation many will partake of the kingdom of God and its new life who do not appear to belong to it; whereas others, who call themselves Christians, will find themselves separated from Jesus when they have to face the truth about themselves in the light of the destiny of man revealed in him (cf. Matt. 25.31–46). Yet it remains a reason for Christian confidence that the future judge is none other than Jesus, on whom the Christian faith already depends. For anyone who receives him is already saved, now, for all eternity: 'He who hears my word and believes him who sent me has eternal life; he does not come into judgment, but has passed from death to life' (John 5.24).

This train of thought is similar to the one followed by the early Christian tradition, when, starting from the expectation that Jesus will come again as judge of the world and end-time ruler of the kingdom of God, it arrived at the conviction that this future event of Jesus' second coming will manifest what is already hidden reality.

The subject of the creed's statement about the risen Jesus' sitting on the right hand of God is this hidden but already exist-ing reality which will become manifest in Jesus' second coming. This statement itself is an allusion to the saying in Psalm 110.1: 'The Lord says to my lord: "Sit at my right hand, till I make your enemies your footstool." ' This saying was originally to be understood as a word of God addressed to the king in Jerusalem and reproduced by the author of the psalm. In it Yahweh prom-ises the king dominion over the world, as he does in Psalm 2.8ff. God himself will lay the king's enemies at his feet. The promised position of power is expressed particularly through the invitation to the king to sit at the right hand of God. In the ancient East, the place at the right hand of the ruler was reserved for the person who was nearest in power to him and who exercised power in his name. When, therefore, God says to the king in

Jerusalem, 'Sit at my right hand', this means that he was giving the king authority to exercise his own rule over the world.

In the primitive church this saying was transferred to Jesus. It was now interpreted as something said by God to Jesus. Perhaps this interpretation was suggested by the text of Psalm 110.1 itself, in the statement that God (the Lord) spoke 'to my lord'. As soon as Jesus was termed 'the Lord' in his church (whatever the sense associated with the title), it seemed obvious to relate the saying in Psalm 110 to him (e.g. Acts 2.34f.). It is more probable, however, that the Messianic faith was the starting point for the Christian interpretation of this psalm. Jewish expectation had already related the psalm to the coming Messiah. If this was the reason for the application of the passage to Jesus, it presupposes that the church expected Jesus to come again, not only as Son of man but also as Messiah, not only as judge of the end-time, but also as king of the future era of salvation. This expectation was, as we saw earlier, suggested by the inscription on the cross, which described Jesus as Messiah. But the deeper reason for the identification of Jesus with the expected Messiah must probably be looked for in the fact that, after the resurrection of Jesus and his fusion with the coming Son of man, there was no room for any other redeeming figure besides, so that the Messianic expectation could also be seen as having been fulfilled in him. The further step to the idea of his sitting at the right hand of God was taken when the *future* world rule of the Messiah was understood as being already existing reality in heaven. What has still to become manifest on earth in the future is only what is already reality in God's eternity. This corresponds to the general Jewish view of the events of the last days: at the end, what is already prepared in heaven – i.e., in God's eternity – will become manifest on earth. So far the step from hope in Jesus as the future Messianic ruler to the acknowledgment that he already reigns now, though in concealment, is an obvious one. Yet the present rule of Christ by no means makes his future rule superfluous, simply because it has still to be revealed on earth in the future, and therefore what is now only reality in divine concealment still has to be implemented.

'Sits at the right hand of God' must not therefore be taken as a spatial statement about the place where the risen Jesus is at the moment. Our spatial standards are not appropriate for the different mode of the resurrection reality. The far-reaching consequences of this problem can be clearly seen when one learns that the spatial understanding of the exaltation of Christ to the right hand of the Father was one of the causes of the dispute about the Lord's Supper between the Zwinglian re- formers and the Lutherans in the sixteenth century. Zwingli maintained that if the body of the risen Lord was to be found spatially (*localiter*) at the right hand of God in heaven, then it could not at the same time be present on earth on the altar. Luther rightly disputed the spatial concept of the sitting at the right hand of God which was implicit in this argument, stressing that the phrase only meant that the risen Jesus is exalted to participation in the almighty power of God, to ex- ercise divine rule over creation.

The briefest reason for acknowledging the rule of Christ is therefore the reference to Jesus' oneness with God. This oneness implies that Jesus partakes of everything which belongs to the Godhead, including its almighty power. The path the early church had to take before arriving at a confession of faith in the rule of Christ was only so much more complicated because the recognition of Jesus' oneness with God was only an ultimate conclusion derived from reflections on the meaning of his resurrection from the dead, and could not yet be presupposed in the primitive church. The fact that the rule of Christ will have no end (which the Nicene Creed expressly adds to its statement about Jesus' coming again to judgment, picking up Luke 1.33) is also a conclusion from Jesus' oneness with God. The kingdom of Christ is identical with the kingdom of God itself; it is not an intermediary state which the kingdom of God will ultimately replace. Paul only seemingly suggests such a view in I Cor. 15.28, when he says that at the end, after everything has been subjected to the Son, the Son himself will be subjected to the Father, so that God may be all in all. This does not mean that the kingdom of Christ and the kingdom of God will succeed one another, as if the duration of the kingdom of Christ were limited. On the contrary, the only significance of the kingdom of Christ itself is to subject everything to the lordship of God and his kingdom. That is what the message of the earthly Jesus was already about: it is completely imbued with the nearness of the kingdom of God and with the urgent exhortation and invitation to men to open their hearts to this nearness.

This already indicates what is to be understood by the lordship of Christ and what its real substance is: the kingdom of Christ is fulfilled when it brings all men – and with men the whole of creation (Rom. 8.21ff.) – into direct, immediate communication with God, when it brings men into the relationship of sonship to God: into the relation to God, that is to say, which was already reality in the earthly existence of Jesus. In this sense one can say with Luther that the lordship of Christ is fulfilled through the preaching of the gospel, and in the union of the hearer of the gospel with Jesus Christ through faith. Through faith, through baptism, and through the Lord's Supper, the hearers of the proclamation of Christ are united with Jesus and are thus drawn into his own relation to God, into his sonship. The real goal of the lordship of God is here shown to be the abolition of the antithesis between ruler and ruled – partici⁄ pation in the glory of God himself. The rule of God is not an end in itself. It has its purpose and its meaning in the love which raises the one who is ruled to itself and makes him capable of liberty.

The rule of Christ is not limited to the church as a special sector within the world of men and human history; through the proclamation of the church, it is directed towards all mankind. Through Jesus and through the message of his church which proceeds from him, the whole world is called into the relation׳ ship to God, its creator, which is its portion. That is why we must not equate the kingdom of Christ with the church. The whole world is God's creation. Consequently the whole world is dependent on God, who unceasingly continues to create it and to perfect his creation. And because all things take their bearings from God, they also take them from Jesus; for Jesus simply reminded the world that it is indebted to its creator alone, and that its creator is also its future. That is why, whether they know it and want it or not, all things and all men are subject to the lordship of Christ, even though they are God's creatures. To this degree Christ's universal rule 'at the right hand of God' is in itself identical with the statement that he is the mediator of creation – the 'only begotten Son'.

But this lordship of Christ, which has its basis in his complete, devoted submission to the Father and to the cause of his coming kingdom, is still a hidden lordship in this present world, just as hidden as the future of the rule of God itself. In the present, only Christians already acknowledge it. Moreover, this acknowledg׳ ment must be more than mere lip׳service. Acknowledgment of the lordship of Christ is unconvincing if it does not determine a Christian's behaviour. It directly implies the practice of faith and love, which in their turn are the foundation of hope, and live from hope. But it is part of the practice of the acknowledg׳ ment of Christ's still׳hidden rule that this should be proclaimed throughout the world, in accordance with the universality of the rule of God and of his Christ. Nor must the factual concealment of the rule of Christ in the present world keep Christians from already living this rule openly and from working at the tasks of human society in accordance with it. Moreover, the hidden character of the rule of Christ will not only show itself in the rejection which the Christian message comes up against; it also means that even the Christian understanding of the meaning of what happened in the history of Jesus constantly proves itself provisional, and hence varying in kind; so that it has to be revised in the light of a better understanding. In the same way all action and endeavour on the part of Christians through which they conform to the rule of Christ always remains provisional and capable of improvement. For we are not yet living in the ultimate reality which has already appeared in Jesus. We live from faith in it, with knowledge which for the time being is provisional and activity which at the best only conforms provisionally to the rule of Christ. But because our knowledge of what happened in Jesus and its meaning remains capable of improvement, and because the Christian proclamation and the actions of Christians therefore also remain capable of improvement, both what Christians say and what they do also run up against opposition in this world, opposition which is, moreover, always at least partially justified. So far the lordship of Christ is not yet manifest even in the church, either in what Christians know or in what they do, or in the character of the church itself. That is why the communion of Christians is still burdened by contrasts in its understanding of the faith and in its behaviour which threaten to tear apart the church's unity. The lordship of Christ is not yet manifest, even in the church, to eyes turned towards what is immediately present; it is only manifest to the faith which confesses Jesus on the basis of what for him has already taken place – for him, but not yet for us.

I Believe in the Holy Spirit

Acknowledgment of the Holy Spirit is not one of the more hotly disputed statements of the Christian tradition today. The reason for this, however, is probably not so much to be sought for in the assumption that the Christian faith enjoys general acceptance at this point; the reason is more probably that talk about the Holy Spirit has become particularly incomprehensible for the present day, and people therefore leave it alone. If one thinks about the reality of the spiritual in general in connection with these words, one immediately becomes involved in the question whether everything spiritual is not only the living expression of conscious beings and only exists for them, whereas the consciousness is to be viewed as a function of material, physical existence, without independent reality apart from those material conditions of life. Moreover, every attempt to understand talk about the Holy Spirit on these lines brings the reproach that one is confusing the Spirit of God with the spirit of man and his creations in art and civilization.

But what is the Spirit of God? Where can we experience it? Is the church and its proclamation in the world to be interpreted as the reality where we have to do with the Holy Spirit? This can mean that the reality of the church is not entirely exhausted by its character as a human institution, with offices developed by men, and human office-bearers, and an often all too human history. In the same way preaching is supposed to be not simply human talk; it is allegedly not only man who is at work in the sacraments; and the Christian's experience of faith is said to be not merely human experience. But if there is a 'more' of reality in all these things, of what does it consist? We are told that it is simply the divine reality of the Holy Spirit. But how is this totally unique kind of reality to be experienced? And in what way can the assertion be justified that in the church we have not only to do with human institutions and human behaviour (as would seem to be the case), but with the divine reality of the Holy Spirit? If we answer that this is what the authority of the church itself and its proclamation tells us, the question then arises: what reason do we have to believe in the authority's trustworthiness in this case, i.e., in the case of this particular assertion; and how can we combat the suspicion that this could be the church's own self-glorification and self-idolization? But if we point to the New Testament as talking about the divine Spirit as the determining reality in the life of the church, then clarification is needed. What did Paul, for example, or the Epistle to the Ephesians mean by this description? What reasons did they have for their opinion? And do these reasons still have the power to convince us or, alternatively, are they to be judged as conditioned by their time, and superseded? If we learn that in the New Testament writings the Spirit has to do with the risen Christ and his continuing presence in his church, the question is both, on what grounds this continuing presence of Christ can be maintained, and also why it is described through the particular concept of the Spirit, and a divine Spirit at that. If we are not willing to content ourselves with pointing to some authority or other, accepting the incomprehensible on the strength of its guarantee, then we shall in any case find ourselves back at the question what the expression 'Holy Spirit' really signifies, and how its application is to be substantially justified. It is only in this way that we can be sufficiently sure whether the expression is more than a meaningless phrase.

The creed drawn up by the Council of Constantinople of 381

adds a series of explanatory statements to the mention of the Holy Spirit, to which the Nicene Creed of 325 had confined itself. The Holy Spirit is described first as the 'giver of life', then the Spirit's unity with the Father and the Son is expressed in several different ways; finally we are told that the Spirit spoke through the prophets. The first of these definitions is also, essentially speaking, the basic one: the Holy Spirit is the origin of life, and in fact the origin of all life.

This most fundamental feature of the biblical notion of the Spirit has become so strange today that one does not even feel the strangeness as disturbing. The emphases, at least, in the doctrine of the Holy Spirit have long encouraged to an increasing degree, even in theology, a curiously watered-down conception of the Spirit: the Holy Spirit is thought of primarily as the principle of the supernatural, above all the supernatural knowledge of faith. The fact that Christian traditions have become increasingly incomprehensible to people in the course of modern times, has all too frequently been countered from the Christian side with the information that nothing else could be expected, since the truths of faith are simply not to be recognized by means of reason, but only through the Holy Spirit. In this way the Holy Spirit increasingly became a mysterious power through which the otherwise incomprehensible, and indeed even the absurd, is nevertheless to be legitimated. This situation only developed in modern times. In the early, and even in the mediaeval, church, the assertions of the Christian faith convinced people through their substance. It was only when Christianity was forced into a defensive position in modern times that people made a spiritual virtue of necessity, making up what the Christian proclamation lacked in power of conviction by a reference to the Holy Spirit. We may well ask ourselves whether this was not an all too easy way of escape from the question which faced the Christian message – the question of what was really true. And has the

Christian doctrine of the Holy Spirit not been misused and discredited because it has been used as a fig-leaf to protect the nakedness of the Christian tradition from the questionings of modern critical thinking? It is of secondary importance here whether this appeal to the Holy Spirit is made in the institutional interests of the church or in the interests of individual piety. It could serve to immunize traditional doctrine against the critical spirit of the modern age without our having to risk coming to terms about the facts with these critical questionings. On the other hand, it served to give Christian devotional experience the consciousness of a superhuman certainty independent of the human plausibility of its substance, which has meanwhile increasingly lost ground. Yet both motives – the concern to secure authority and the concern of pious experience for an absolute certainty, such as the search for plausible human reasons cannot really guarantee – have united in a formal faith in authority. But in the conditions of modern times this faith in authority is no longer covered by the objective power of the ecclesiastical institution; it now finds its basis in its apparent opposite, namely in the subjectivistic arbitrariness with which the irrational need for complete certainty – a certainty capable of putting down doubt once and for all – submits to this or that claim to absolute authority. The desire that what one believes should be absolutely certain is a latent hotbed of authoritarian views and fanaticism; and the content of these differing tendencies has often shown itself as being interchangeable to an astonishing degree.

Today it is time to see through this need for certainty as being in itself misguided, and to distinguish the false desire for objective certainty, which can only be satisfied by belief in authority, from the trusting certainty of faith, which consists of the total committal of one's own existence in the act of trust, but which is not capable of extending the theoretical credibility of the substance of faith into an absolute theoretical certainty. It is part of the situation of the 'pilgriming' church, which has not yet reached the final consummation, that the content of faith should remain exposed to doubt. It is part of the provisional nature of Christian existence. Standing firm in this situation means to content ourselves soberly with the rational plausibility of what has been passed down to us, which will always be only a qualified plausibility, and not to escape out of this situation by a desire for a supernatural, absolute certainty. It is part of faith's situation to expose the very substance of what it believes to the experience of the future, which the believer expects will be God's future. This makes the Christian capable of dialogue. He does not need to shut himself up into his own subjective convictions by giving them absolute validity, as the workings of the Holy Spirit. His very consciousness of the provisional nature of his conviction of faith, its openness for the divine future, could be the expression of the presence of the divine Spirit.

Spiritual subjectivism, in which appeal to the Spirit is to guarantee the otherwise unattainable absolute certitude of personal experience, has its origin among the 'Enthusiasts' of the Reformation period and their pietistic heirs. At that time the issue was the inwardness of faith, as distinct from external doctrinal authority. And that is the element of truth in this subjective attitude to the Spirit. Consequently it was not by chance that it had a profound influence on the thinking of modern times, down to German ninteenth-century Idealism. On the other hand, it cannot invoke Luther. For Luther subordinated the Spirit to the Word; it is only through the external Word of the message of Christ that the true Spirit is received, and the Spirit adds nothing to that message. For Luther, the Word of the Bible and the Word as it is preached contains its own inherent truth, although of course not everyone will recognize this truth. For that, there must indeed be illumin-ation, so that the Word of the message of Christ may dawn for the individual. It must touch him inwardly and overcome his deeply-rooted prejudices. This illumination is the work of the Spirit, which proceeds from the Word. For Luther, however, the Word of Scripture quite simply still contained its own inherent truth. What it has to tell was not for Luther a basically neutral history, to which the hearer's own opinion must be added as an appendage, which must then in its turn be sub- stantiated through an additional principle, the Holy Spirit, since the content of the message is not a substantiation in itself. This interpretation only became the prevailing one in the course of the ninteenth century. And through it – by viewing the Holy Spirit as a kind of supernatural key to a Christian message which has meanwhile become incomprehensible – the original breadth of the efficacy of the Spirit in the sense of the Bible and the Christian tradition has, as we have said, been forgotten or at least pushed into the background.

In the Old Testament the Spirit was by no means primarily a source of supernatural knowledge; it was above all the origin of all life. In this context the idea of the Spirit is closely con- nected with wind, air and breath. It is Psalm 104 which probably describes most impressively the enlivening effects of the divine Spirit. 'When thou hidest thy face, they are dismayed; when thou takest away their breath, they die and return to their dust. When thou sendest forth thy Spirit, they are created; and thou renewest the face of the ground' (Ps. 104.29f.). The same fundamental view lies behind the account of creation in the Priestly Document, which begins by telling how the stormy wind of the divine Spirit brings movement out of chaos (Gen. 1.2). And according to the description of the older account of creation in the second chapter of the Bible, man, having once been formed from earth, is quickened into life because God breathes on him (Gen. 2.7). The extraordinary (charismatic) powers which are ascribed to the Spirit of God in particular cases are also to be understood in the light of this general efficacy of the divine Spirit as the origin of all life: these are special, unusual capacities and attainments, which demand a particular degree of vital energy, a special infusion of the creative spirit of God. They are to be found among heroes and prophets, but also among musicians, poets and artists. In all these cases men have to do with a particular operation of the same power which is the origin of all life.

These biblical ideas make it clear how far our contemporary theology is from a doctrine of the Holy Spirit which corresponds to the breadth of the biblical statements about that Spirit. For this, theological penetration into the biological phenomenon of life would seem to be necessary. But what point would there be in talking about the 'spiritual' origin of all life in connection with the living phenomena which biology has explored? One would have to be able to show that, in order to understand the phenomenon of life, talk of the Spirit of God is indispensable. This would be the only way to attack the problem of a theological doctrine of the Holy Spirit with a breadth of vision corresponding to that of the biblical tradition. The difficulties, if we map out the task in this way, are obvious, in face of what is known about life today. The science of biology interprets the phenomena of life immanently as functions of living cells. In the thinking of the ancient Israelites, on the other hand, the origin of life was thought of as a living power transcending the living being: this is what is meant by the idea of the divine Spirit.

But is this obvious contrast in the understanding of the phenomenon of life really not bridged by any analogy? Are living things, according to today's view, dependent in no way at all on a reality which surmounts them – dependent, moreover, for the actual fulfilment of their lives? It is obvious that such dependencies do exist. Every organism, if it is to bring its life to fulfilment, needs an appropriate environment, in which it can feed, develop and reproduce. Moreover, environments are not completely self-contained. They have a temporal as well as a spatial structure. A living being's behaviour towards his environment is at the same time his behaviour towards the fulfilment and alteration of his own existence in the future. The temporal aspect becomes even more relevant when the environ-ments of species are related to the process of their evolution. Thus every organism lives beyond the thing that it already is. Man's openness to the world is only a new stage in this self-transcend-ence of all life. And the ecstatic nature of all spiritual experience forms yet another modification of the fundamental fact that everthing living only acquires present fulfilment of life by rising above itself. Artistic inspiration; a sudden flash of illumin-ation through a long sought after, or perhaps a surprising, chance insight; the uplifting impulse which binds individuals together in moral aspiration – in all this we should then have to recognize particular forms of manifestation of the self-transcend-ence which is the mark of everything that lives. What is ex-perienced in a special way in these highest forms of spiritual experience would have to be understood as characteristic of all life: everything living lives through participation in a reality which supersedes it and which escapes final fixation by its openness towards what is ahead.

These reflections may perhaps offer a new way of access to the essence of the spiritual: spirit would then not have to be under-stood from the aspect of consciousness and from the subjectivity of the self-consciousness, but the consciousness would on the contrary appear as the expression of a particular stage in a living thing's participation in the spiritual reality which is at work in the self-transcendence of everything living. First tentative attempts at an understanding of life which takes its bearings in this way, in the context of the Spirit, can be found in Teilhard de Chardin, even if there it is still much too closely confined by the usual

identification of spirit and consciousness. Such attempts probably still need a long period of revision and have to be thoroughly
explored theoretically and empirically before it would be possible
to talk about a solid basis for the view of life in the context of the
Spirit which we have only touched on here as a possibility – a
view of life which might be capable of absorbing the intentions
of the old Israelite view of life and spirit, under the conditions
of modern biological research into the phenomenon of life, and
which would thereby provide a horizon of understanding for a
theological doctrine of the Holy Spirit.

In the context of the ancient Israelite views about life and
spirit, it is possible to understand what is meant by the Israelite
expectation that the Spirit of God would become active in a
particular way in the end-time. According to Isa. 11.2 the
Messiah will not only be led by the Spirit, but he will partake of
that Spirit permanently; the Spirit will rest on him. The Second
Isaiah promised not only the king but the whole people of
Israel that the Spirit of God would be conferred on them in a
new way in the end-time (Isa. 42.1; 44.3). A similar promise is
to be found in Ezekiel as well (36.27). In the last of his night
visions, Zechariah even saw the Spirit of God descending on all
nations: like chariots, the winds drive the Spirit (*ruach*) of
Yahweh into the four corners of heaven, over the whole earth
(Zech. 6.1–8). Finally, the prophet Joel also promised that the
Spirit of God would be poured out on 'all flesh' at the end-
time (Joel 3.1ff.). And in the early Christian period Luke
found this prophecy fulfilled in the events of Pentecost (Acts 2.
17ff.). In all these Old Testament sayings the Spirit of God is
understood as the power of life, not primarily as the source of
knowledge not to be acquired in any other way. Wisdom and
knowledge are certainly only vouchsafed through the Spirit of
love. But there we are not dealing with something unusual or
supernatural; for the same applies to all the phenomena of life in

general. Every living phenomenon is in its unique character a special manifestation of the Spirit of God.

For Israel, the difference between the future, end-time activity of the Spirit and its present activity was that in the end-time the Spirit will be poured out – that it will rest on men; in short, that it will be appropriated by them entirely and inalienably. This is connected with the fact that the life of the end-time is bound to be a different and more intense life than the mortal life which we lead now. Our present life is mortal because in it men have not remained united to the origin of that life, which is the Spirit of God. That origin remains external to this present life, for life has detached itself from its origin. Consequently, although as creatures men can certainly be led by the Spirit, the Spirit is not vouchsafed to them, in the sense of inner appropriation – or at least not permanently.

The Old Testament conception of the Spirit of God as the power of life makes it possible for us to understand the close connection which exists for the primitive church between the Spirit and the new reality of the life of the resurrection which has appeared in Jesus – the life for which Christians also hope, and in which they even begin to partake already, in so far as they are united with Jesus. Since the Spirit is the origin of all life, it is even more the origin of the new life of the resurrection of the dead: it is not by chance that Paul says that it was the Spirit through whom Jesus was raised (Rom. 1.4; 8.2, 11). But more: the life-giving principle of the divine Spirit not only created the life of the resurrection; it also remains bound up with it. The life of the raised differs from our present earthly life in that it is entirely permeated by the Spirit, as the creative origin of life. This corresponds in an amazing way to the Israelite-Jewish expectation that at the end-time the Spirit of God would rest on men. So when in I Cor. 15.44f. Paul talks about a spiritual body (*soma pneumatikon*) in order to describe the unique nature of the resurrection life, this is a significant and highly pregnant formulation, and by no means the rather clumsy and vague way of expressing himself which has often been supposed. What he means is a life which remains bound to the divine origin of all life and which is therefore not delivered over to death but is everlasting, immortal (15.52f.). The second, final man is not merely a 'living soul'; he is himself a life-giving spirit (15.45). Thus the resurrection reality and the Holy Spirit belong indissolubly together.

Because the new, everlasting life of the resurrection of the dead has already appeared in Jesus, the Spirit of God is also present for men through him. That is why all theologically pregnant statements about the Spirit in Paul are related to Christ and take a christological form. The same is true in John (John 14. 26; 16.31f.). It is only possible to talk appropriately about the Spirit of God in reference to the risen Christ, in connection with the new reality of life which has already appeared in Jesus. But Christ and the Spirit also belong together in a converse sense. Where life is in any way related to the risen Christ, the Spirit is there as well; that is why anyone who listens to the message of the raising of Jesus is already in the Spirit's sphere of activity. And the man who believes the message of the resur- rection of Jesus has thereby already received the Spirit, who vouches for the believer's own future resurrection from the dead because he has already raised Jesus. 'If the Spirit of him who raised Jesus from the dead dwells in you, he who raised Christ Jesus from the dead will give life to your mortal bodies also through his Spirit which dwells in you' (Rom. 8.11). The Spirit dwells in Christians through the message of the risen Jesus and through faith in this message. Anyone who accepts the message of the risen Christ, believing that he will share in the reality which has already appeared in Jesus, has, like all others who are united with Jesus, already with that message received the Holy Spirit.

He is already assured of the new life. In his self-understanding he is no longer subject to death; he has already reached beyond his own death. In what he thinks and does he is free from the death to which human existence is otherwise universally subject. For death calls everything in question; all the standards and values of human life lose their validity in the face of life's subjection to death. Only hope in a life after death liberates from this futility. That is the reason for the specifically Christian serenity in the face of life's transitoriness. It is also the basis for the specific Christian possibility of detaching oneself from one's own self-centredness and yielding oneself up in one's behaviour to the workings of the love of God. In this way the Spirit is the first-fruits of future salva- tion (Rom. 8.23), the foretaste of the new life, a foretaste which lives in hope and believing trust, anticipating the future, even now, in our present existence, in spite of its subjection to death.

The relation of the Spirit to the future of God gives life in the Spirit a prophetic character. Where the Spirit is at work, every- thing is full of pointers towards the future fulfilment of human destiny in a new life. That is why the Niceno-Constantinopolitan Creed rightly stresses the connection of the Spirit with prophecy. It identifies the Spirit as the one 'who spake by the prophets'. This means the Old Testament prophets in the first instance, and again links up the Christian faith with the divine history of Israel. The reality of the divine Spirit which was to reveal itself in the future was already at work in what the Old Testament prophets said, long before it appeared in Jesus. In that the prophets witnessed to the future consummation, the Spirit spoke through them. But then the same applies to the early Christian gift of prophecy. And in this sense all Christian living and speaking in the Spirit has something of the prophetic about it. By the same definition, the creative working of the Spirit as the origin of everything, including the life of the present, would also have to be understood in the light of the future. The Spirit confers their future on all created things and thereby gives them life.

The Spirit is at work in Christians through their faith in Jesus: through the trust that Jesus will abide by the communion he has promised to all who confess him. The presence of the Spirit expresses itself in the trust that the reality of life which has appeared in Jesus will also be manifest in them; the Spirit is therefore already present in Christians through faith and hope. The Spirit is the assurance of being united with Jesus and with his life, which overcomes death – an assurance which is not theoretical but is the assurance of trust. Through communion with Jesus the Spirit also opens up communion with God: Christians are the 'sons of God' in so far as they are filled with his Spirit (Gal. 4.6; Rom. 8.14). Because the Spirit who appeared and proved mighty in Jesus is the Spirit of God himself, he is a bond with God inasmuch as he is a bond with Jesus. He makes believers 'sons of God', just as Jesus was the Son of God, but through participation in Jesus and through the mediation of the message about him. The Spirit, therefore, is the ground for the sending of Christians into the world, as Jesus himself was sent.

The Spirit is the present reality of God, the mode of the presence of the God of Jesus, whose power and kingdom is still to come, yet has already come to us in the sending of Jesus. In that Jesus proclaimed God as the one that is to come, as the God of the coming kingdom – proclaimed him in such a way that he pledged everything to that future – the future of God already became the present for his disciples; for it became for them the unlimited power which determines the present. To an even greater extent, the church of Jesus experienced the appearances of the risen Christ as the dawn of the future of God, as the beginning of God's kingdom. But the process of history taught that the presence of God in Jesus was still, for the moment, confined to this one person. In him the God who was to come had already come to the world of men, once, in a piece of history which had now been completed. But he did not leave his church behind, empty and alone, in the history that followed. The God of Jesus remained present in the church in the experience of the Spirit, through whom the creator is already present among his creatures in the breath of life which they owe to him. But the divine Spirit is otherwise only present to created beings in in- spiration's ecstatic experience of the future fulfilment of existence – with clear awareness in the inspiration of the prophets and concentrated into the promised future's present realization in the life and ministry of Jesus. For the Christian church, however, the Spirit of God is present through the mediation of a past history, namely the story of Jesus, which is so filled with the Spirit of the coming God that its proclamation bestows a share in the presence of God which was once realized in it. Because the presence of the Spirit is not mediated to the Christian church through direct intuition of the one who is to come, but through the past of Jesus, the Spirit is given to the church as a permanent possession, poured out into the hearts of its members through faith and hope.

Through faith and hope – for the point at issue is, after all, the presence of God's future, which has already arrived in the story of Jesus, to which the Christian church looks back. But because the Spirit is the mode of the presence of the coming God, who has already come in Jesus, his presence among believers does not yet find its fulfilment and consummation in faith and hope *per se*, but in the love which lives out of faith and hope. With the courage of faith which reaches beyond everything that exists in the present, and accompanied by the hope for the thing towards which it is directed, love as Christianity has discovered it since Jesus is creative love – prodigal virtue, as Nietzsche so beautifully put it, without knowing that he was describing the unique character of love in the Christian sense. Love is creative to the degree to which it is independent of the beloved's already existing merits, because it itself creates what it loves. Thus the love of the good Samaritan is creative love which turns to the needy man who is not yet his neighbour but who becomes so through the Samaritan's helpfulness (Luke 10.36f.).

But such love is not the act of the loving person alone. The loving person finds himself raised above himself in the act of loving. Love shares this ecstatic feature with other forms of spiritual life, such as the emotion that comes with perception or artistic inspiration. The special thing about love here is that it raises men above themselves to participation in the eternal being of God himself. Through love man partakes in the creative dynamic of the divine love. For as creative love, the God of the future is turned towards, and present in, the world which he has already created – turned towards it and present in it as the world which he has still to perfect. But the divine love finds its fulfil-ment in the fact that God's future is not only to come, but has already come, in the story of Jesus Christ. Thus in the event of love the future of God is bound up with the past of his having-come and is, proceeding from both, living present. Love reveals that the God who is love is himself present in the activity of the Spirit. That is why the ancient church was able to perceive that the Holy Spirit was one with the Father and the Son in the unity of the one divine reality. In the Spirit which proceeds from the risen Christ and is mediated through the Christian proclama-tion, that same God is present whom Jesus preached as the Father of the coming kingdom and who through this witness was present in Jesus as the 'Son'. That is why the Constantino-politan expansion of the Nicene Creed of 381 says that the Spirit is of one nature with the Father and the Son and is with the Father and the Son equally worshipped and glorified. The three persons of the Father, the Son and the Spirit are indisso-lubly bound together in the unity of the divine love. The future of the coming God is present through the Spirit of love who, as the completion of the divine being, is and remains accessible to men through the ministry and the life, death and resurrection of Jesus.

The Holy Catholic Church,
The Communion of Saints

The Apostles' Creed is one of the early Christian credal texts which is divided on Trinitarian lines. Its statements are linked with the three forms of the God of love revealed through Jesus Christ. The baptismal candidate who professed the faith of the church in the words of the Apostles' Creed, and the Christian who renews that profession today in the services of the church, thereby not only repeat certain statements of the church's tradition; through these statements they acknowledge the personal reality of the triune God in the sense in which we use the word when we talk about acknowledging someone in other connections: we are uniting our destiny with his. We do not do this by our own authority, but in endorsement of God's acknowledgment of mankind, as this took shape in the life, death and resurrection of Jesus and as it has been conferred on us through the mediation of the church in baptism. Because the Trinitarian division of the credal statements (which ultimately goes back to the baptismal charge in Matt. 28.19) expresses this personal meaning of the confession of faith, it is theologically right that it should have won its way, over against differently divided early Christian credal formulations. Credal formulae with five divisions have come down to us from Egypt and Ethiopia; these go back to a second-century creed which originated in Asia Minor and, besides Father, Son and Spirit, name the church as well as the forgiveness of sins (which was directly associated with the act of baptism) or the Christian hope for the resurrection of the dead. Now it was not that the third century baptismal creed of the church in Rome, which was later expanded into its present form as the Apostles' Creed, neglected these tenets of faith for the sake of concentrating on the Trinity; it absorbed them into its text and assigned them to the third article, the acknowledgment of the Holy Spirit. This is an expression of the close relationship between the Spirit and the church, the forgiveness of sins received in baptism and the Christian hope, even though these statements were originally independent themes.

Assigning the acknowledgment of the church to the third article means that the present structures of the church are a part of the creed in the light of their divine determination, as the sphere of the Spirit which proceeds from Jesus Christ and which is poured out upon believers. The Roman catechism of 1564 in its textual version of the Apostles' Creed here rightly distinguished the acknowledgment of the church as a *credo ecclesiam* from the immediately preceeding confession of faith 'in' the Holy Spirit (*credo* in *Spiritum Sanctum*). The Christian does not believe 'in' the church (in the sense of *credere in*), as he believes in God, in his threefold reality as Father, Son and Spirit. But he acknow‹ ledges the church in spite of its faults and deficiencies: he acknowledges the church as the field of activity of the Spirit of Christ.

This perspective is brought out by the earliest predicate (already attested in the second century) which the creed as‹ sociates with the mention of the church: the church's holiness describes its separation from the profane world and the fact that it belongs to God and to his activity in the world. According to biblical tradition, everything is holy which belongs to the divine sphere and which is allied to it because it has been chosen by God. It is in accordance with the Christian belief in the incarnation, moreover, that holiness does not mean separation from the world but that the church should be sanctified in the midst of the world for God and his coming.

The church's unity belongs together with its holiness, and this was especially stressed in the Nicene Creed and in other fourth-century Greek credal formulations. The unity of all Christians in the one church is not, as it were, an undoubtedly desirable goal, whose realization can easily be assigned to an indefinite point in the future without any harm to Christianity; the church in the fullest sense of the word is not realized at all without the unity of all Christians. Its holiness as the church of the one God and the one Lord Jesus Christ demands its unity, and demands it unconditionally. At this point, in view of the denominational divisions of Christianity, the contrast between the way in which the creed talks about the church and the existing conditions of our ecclesiastical organization is especially crass. This does not mean that the true church would be invisible and only live in the hearts of believers. It belongs to the essence of the Christian church, as the community of the incarnate God, to take on physical shape in institutional form. And Christianity has fought incessantly throughout the course of its history to acquire such a form. At certain times it has been more con-vincingly successful than at others; at times the essence of the church and the divine love for mankind which is at work in the community of its members has been obscured by divisions among Christians or by other perversions of the Christian way of life. The contrast between the acknowledgment of the unity of the church and the actually existing divisions of Christendom shows that the church of faith has only inadequately taken shape in the present state of our ecclesiastical institutions and needs to represent the communion of all Christians more clearly and appropriately; and this is the goal of the great ecumenical move-ments of the present time.

The general, or catholic, nature of the church is deeply linked with its unity. The Greek word 'catholic' means universal, and Protestants should also be able to acknowledge the universality of the church. The church is indeed only a single and particular institution among other institutions of society, and it always only numbers a part of mankind among its members. But it is of decisive importance that, though factually limited, it is open to the needs and destiny of all mankind in all the different facets of their spheres of living. The universality of the church urges the existing churches to look towards the whole of mankind, beyond the limitations of a narrow ecclesiasticism but also beyond the bounds of nation, race and class, and to live for peace and justice among all men. The concept of the catholic, universal church (which goes back to the second century) was adopted into the creeds of the ancient church in the fourth century. It is a matter of regret that, in the sixteenth-century Protestant confessional documents, this attribute of the church was pushed aside in the translation of the Apostles' and Nicene creeds, being replaced by the term 'Christian church'. The creeds are still repeated in this form in many church services even today, in Germany and elsewhere. In actual fact, however, the church needs the universal gaze outwards, to the whole of mankind, for whom God's will towards reconciliation holds good; it needs it as the standard for its self-understanding today at least as much as at any earlier time, even beyond the ecumenical unity of Christians.

It is only as the catholic, universal church that the Christian church can also be apostolic in the sense of the fourth predicate and criterion of the church named in the Nicene Creed. In the Apostles' Creed this attribute is not expressly mentioned. But the universality of the church and its faithfulness to its apostolic mission belong together, because the mission of the apostles was directed towards the whole of mankind, in the name of the one

God of all men, to whom the risen Christ had been exalted – the Christ who sent out the apostles. The apostolic character of the church does not depend on its preserving the conditions and modes of thought of the apostolic era in as unaltered a form as possible, many though the generations of Christians may be who have believed this. Alteration is unavoidable in the process of history. What is decisive is that the church clings to and pursues the apostles' *mission* to the whole of mankind. This mission cannot be left to 'foreign' missionaries, as a special task. It must permeate every manifestation of the church's life. At the same time this Christian mission to mankind emits a dynamic im⁄ pulse for the alteration both of 'the world' and of the church itself. Thus the permanent identity of the church and its alteration are united in the process of its mission.

The church has four classical 'attributes': it is holy, united, catholic and apostolic. But these are not the characteristics of an existing and already perfected institution; they are the criteria of a missionary movement in which the church strives to realize its essence, which is also its destiny. But are these criteria an ex⁄ haustive description of the church's unique nature? Do they not rather already presuppose a 'something' which is by definition holy, united, universal and in accordance with its apostolic mission – by its definition which is, rather, its destiny? The need for a closer explanatory definition of the concept of the church was already felt even during the time of the early church. That was the reason why the phrase 'the communion of saints' was added to the Apostles' Creed. We first come across the addition towards the end of the four century in Serbia; it then came into general use in Gaul, and was finally included in the ancient baptismal creed in Rome as well. In more recent times its mean⁄ ing has been much puzzled over. Two differing interpretations are possible.

In the Protestant churches since the sixteenth century, the

prevailing view has been that the saints, whose communion is referred to, are Christians; this is in accordance with New Testament usage (Rom. 1.7; I Cor. 1.2; II Cor. 1.1; Eph. 1.1; Phil. 1.1; Col. 1.2; and frequently elsewhere). The communion of saints would accordingly mean the communion of Christians, and the concept of the church would therefore be being characterized in the Apostles' Creed by the fact that Christians constitute a joint community. The basic definition of the concept of the church in the Augsburg Confession of 1530 accordingly runs: the church is the assembly of the saints (*congregatio sanctorum*). For Luther and the other reformers this phrase meant the same as the assembly of believers (*congregatio fidelium*). Thus the German version of the statement in the Augsburg Confession which we have just quoted states that the church is the '*Versammlung aller Gläubigen* – the assembly of all believers (CA VII). The next article of the Augsburg Confession also calls the church the 'assembly of all believers and saints'.

The original meaning of the phrase 'communion of saints', however, points in another direction. What was originally meant was not the coming together of believers for communion with one another but, on the one hand, communion with the holy martyrs (who already partake of divine salvation in heaven and are hence coguarantors of the future participation in salvation of all Christians); on the other hand, the formula was understood in the sense of participation in the '*sancta*' – the sacraments, which link Christians with eternal salvation. It seems obvious here to think particularly of the eucharist, which was the centre of the worshipping life of the ancient church. The two interpretations of '*sancta*', as applying to the martyrs and to the sacraments, must be viewed as having equally primal force. The additional phrase 'the communion of saints' therefore describes the church as the institution in which one participates in the divine mysteries which mediate salvation and in which one has communion with the martyrs who are already partakers in salvation. The extension of the latter, personal meaning of *communio sanctorum* to all Christians, as the Reformed interpretation expressed it, is a further development which is intelligible from the association of the formula in the creed with the Pauline description of all Christians as 'called to be saints'.

The idea of participation in the holy, the *sancta*, in the sacramental sense, has not in itself simply disappeared in the Reformed understanding of the church either. The Augsburg Confession does not content itself with characterizing the church as the assembly of the saints (or believers); it goes on: 'among whom the gospel is purely preached and the holy sacraments administered in accordance with the gospel.' In the Reformed sense, the preaching of the gospel and the distribution of the sacraments give what the ancient formula calls 'participation in the holy'; that is to say, the participation of believers in salvation. For the real meaning of sacramental communion is participation in Jesus Christ himself, which is mediated through the eucharist as it has already been mediated through baptism. And anyone who is united with Jesus Christ has the hope of partaking in the salvation which has appeared in his resurrection from the dead. To mediate to men communion with Christ and the salvation which has appeared in him: this is the definition of the church in the Reformed interpretation as well. That is the purpose of preaching and the sacraments alike. In this the Reformation agrees with the ancient church. What is noticeable about the formulations of the Augsburg Confession, as distinct from that of the Apostles' Creed, is merely that preaching is expressly mentioned beside, or rather before, the sacraments. This makes it clear that the churches of the Reformation understand themselves as being in a particular way churches of the Word. On the other hand we must note that even in the creeds of the ancient church, where – if at all – only the sacraments were mentioned, the concept of the sacrament had then, and right down to the Middle Ages, a wider sense than it has today: it was not only a case of particular ecclesiastical rites; until the height of the Middle Ages, the whole content of the faith could be summed up in the concept of the sacraments – the 'divine mysteries'. As late as the twelfth century, Hugh of Saint-Victor wrote a dogmatic treatise in Paris with the title 'On the Mysteries of the Christian Faith' (*De sacramentis christianae fidei*). Here the rites of the church appear in the context of the mysteries of salvation history, through which God brought about the salvation of mankind. Participation 'in the holy' therefore means participation in the divine mysteries of salvation, which are available to mankind through Jesus Christ and whose real sense is communion with him, and through him with God.

Our previous discussion about the phrase 'communion of saints' suggested that the church must be understood primarily as the communion with Christ which is mediated through preaching and the ordinances of the church, which guarantee the individual communion with Jesus Christ. To this general Christian understanding of the church as the mediator of participation in Jesus Christ and in the salvation accomplished by him, the Reformers added the church's hall-mark as the assembly of believers. This bears a specifically Protestant stress. It is not primarily the hierarchy of bishops and other office-bearers that constitutes the church; the church's centre of gravity lies in its character as the assembly of all believers. The priest-hood of all believers is its basis. It is true that according to the Lutheran interpretation it also needs the office of the ministry – the ministry of preaching initiated by God to gather the com-munity of believers (CA V), as it has done since the time of the apostles. It is only through this that faith can come into being. The ministry of preaching is there to mediate communion with Christ, and through communion with Christ believers are in their turn joined together in communion with one another. Communion with Christ and the communion of believers with one another belong inalienably together.

The interrelation between communion with Christ and the communion of Christians with one another describes the inmost essence of the church. But this hallmark is open to misinterpretation in the sense of an exclusively private, inner devotionalism, withdrawn from the world. It is open to this misinterpretation as long as we ignore the horizon to which Jesus' message and ministry was related, and to which consequently Christ's communion of believers must also be related if it is really to be in communion with Jesus. This horizon is the horizon of the future of God, the expectation of God's coming kingdom. With this the original sense of the word church (*ekklesia*) emerges, and its relationship to the Old Testament idea of the community chosen by God, to whom the promises of God apply (I Kings 8.55). The early church's description of itself as *ekklesia* is an expression of its understanding of itself as the heir of the promises to Israel. The church knew itself to be God's community of the end-time. As such the ground of its existence lies in the expectation of God's final coming, in the proclamation of his coming rule and its dawn with Jesus as his Messiah. What the church means as communion with Christ and participation in the holy can only be properly described in this context.

The church is not the kingdom of God. The kingdom of God is, rather, the church's future as it is the future of the world. It is true that since Augustine the church has been equated with the kingdom of *Christ*, linking on to the Jewish-Christian expectation of the Messiah's thousand-year empire before the dawn of the end and the kingdom of God. Augustine purified this chiliastic idea from all its end-time drama by equating the kingdom of the Messiah with the age of the church. But this identification of the two is problematical also; for the kingdom of God and the kingdom of Christ are not to be separated, and both signify the future towards which the church moves. Yet the future of Christ as the Lord of the church already determines the church's present as well. The rule of Christ is in fact already present in the church's proclamation. For the rule of Christ can have no different goal from his earthly ministry, where it was to call men into the kingdom of God and to proclaim the coming of that kingdom. Through the continuation of the mission of Jesus Christ in the church's proclamation of Christ, the rule of Christ shows itself to be present within it. And yet the community of Christians in the particular historical form which its life takes at any given time is not identical with the kingdom of Christ. The kingdom of God and of his Christ is greater than the church.

Because the kingdom of God is the future of the church, as well as the future of the world, the church finds itself united with human society and the whole world of men in the expectation of God's coming rule. The relevance of society for the self-understanding of the church is founded on its relation to the future of God's kingdom. Participation in the holy is not to be won through other-worldly confinement to a religious sphere which leaves the world of society to itself.

The expectation of a future divine kingdom which will replace and end the series of world empires, developed in ancient Israel in connection with the hope of a future kingdom of peace in which righteousness and humanity would reign. That is why the future kingdom of God is symbolized in the book of Daniel by the figure of a man (Dan. 7.13) instead of by the beast figures which characterize the nature of the world empires of the ancient East. The church, as the community of the end-time, is now the company of people who are already united in expectation of God's future for mankind. The relation of the church to Jesus

Christ also belongs within this context of hope for the kingdom of God. For Jesus became the origin of the church by proclaim, ing unconditional trust in the future of the kingdom of God as the first, only and all-embracing condition of final salvation. As a community of people encouraged by Jesus to unconditional trust in the future of the rule of God, the Christian church continues the history of the Israelite-Jewish community, inas, much as it, too, was already moulded by hope in the future of God and his kingdom. But this hope has now, through Jesus, become the sole and wholly sufficient basis for the relationship to God in general. With this the limits of the Israelite national community have been burst apart: it is no longer the special Israelite traditions which are constitutive for membership of the church but simply hope in the future rule of God as Jesus had proclaimed it and as that rule, through Jesus, already determines the present. That is why the church is the new people of God drawn from all nations. In the history of Christendom this has frequently, and with disastrous consequences, been understood as an antithesis to the election of Israel, as if that were now rescinded. Yet Paul expressly says that God has not rejected his people (Rom. 11.1). The Christian church is not the new people of God in contrast to Israel. On the contrary, it has been grafted into the olive tree of Israel (Rom. 11.17f.). But through the church of Christ the history of Israel's election has been ex, tended to the whole of mankind.

As the community of those who, being united with Jesus, wait for the future of God and live their present lives from this expectation, the church is the beginning of a new mankind, which already lays hold of and embodies for all men man's destiny in the face of God's future and his will of love. In this way the church is related to the coming kingdom of God: the kingdom of God is not the church; it is the future of the church, as it is the future of all mankind. But the church is the com, munity of those who already wait for the kingdom of God for Jesus' sake and live from this expectation. The definition of the church as communion with Christ also has its location in the context of the hope of the kingdom of God. Communion with Christ is misinterpreted when it is understood as the goal of an aloof and egotistical striving for personal salvation on the part of the pious. Whenever the horizon of the kingdom of God has been forgotten in an understanding of the church as communion with and in Christ, the result has been the narrow piety of a mystery society which shuns the world, a society for the joint cossetting of religious needs or a clerical institution for the transmission of salvation. Only a relation to the future of the coming kingdom of God, surmounting the narrowness of its internal ecclesiastical interests, can make the church conscious of its importance for the world – that is to say, its importance for mankind as a whole. Questions of the political and social organization of the human community are not the least important in this connection; for hope of the kingdom of God has always, since its Old Testament beginnings, been directed towards peace and righteousness and hence towards a truly human way of living together. Within the orbit of its historical sphere of activity, therefore, the church can never fail to be interested in the question of justice and of the political and social order of society. On the contrary, it will strive to see something of the future destiny of man taking shape in the due order of presentday society, something which will find its ultimate fulfilment in the coming kingdom of God.

Since it looks for the coming rule of God, however, the church will not be able to hold any present form of organized or individual life to be final, but will see every positive achievement only as a provisional stage which must be left behind once more and which is in addition threatened by the dangers of retrogression and decay. This leads our argument back to the criterion of the church's holiness, which now takes on new meaning in the context of hope for the kingdom of God.

It became plain earlier that the holiness of the church denotes its bond with God and his cause in the world. For holy does not mean 'morally irreproachable'; it means 'set aside'. God is holy in his separation from the world, in the sublime transcendence of his freedom as regards the world. God's love is holy love because it comes from the freedom of God and draws man, to whom it is directed, out of the world into communion with the holy God. The church is holy because it is separated from the existing world, being bound up with the future of God and his kingdom. The consciousness of the provisional nature of everything that exists, even all Christian forms of living, is the reverse side of this turning towards the future of God. On the other hand, in view of the special nature of the holiness of the God of the Bible, the holiness of the church cannot mean separation from the world; for the God of the Bible is holy in his love, in the coming of his kingdom in this world and for this world. That is why the holiness of the Church is also fulfilled in Christian love. But that very love is connected with consciousness of the provisional nature of all finite reality, finding through that very consciousness power for creative renewal. The church must be conscious of the provisional nature of everything finite, even and especially in respect of its own form, its own order and even its own doctrine. The holiness of the church includes the necessity for constantly renewed reformation – reformation not as the pruning away of what has grown up historically on the top of Christianity's original historical structure, but as a renewal which looks forward to the future of the rule of God, which has been already opened up through Jesus' message and his life, death and resurrection.

A glance back at the history of the church only lets us see the tokens of its holiness in blurred and distorted form. This history has been all too deeply marked by the fact that the church has on the one hand separated itself from the world in an often sterile way; but on the other hand in its doctrine and order it has settled down in the world, as if for ever, and has failed to remind the world of its provisional nature. Above all, however, the church has itself all too often made use of the forms and methods of human domination, even down to bloody violence. And it has constantly compromised itself by helping, knowingly or unknowingly, to stabilize even inhuman conditions by the cultivation of an other-wordly piety. The holiness of the church only becomes evident where the creative impulse of love is joined to awareness of the provisional and passing nature of all earthly things in the light of the future of the rule of God.

The provisional nature of the present world is also the only reason for the continued existence of the church as a separate institution apart from the political and social order of human society. When the kingdom of God has been fulfilled, its new Jerusalem will have no further need of any special religious institution or temple (Rev. 21.22). Then all life will be carried on in the light of the direct presence of God. But in the present world, man's destined communion with God still requires a special institution devoted to this cause, because the life of men is still alienated from its divine destiny. A special religious institution is therefore only needed because the destiny of man is not yet realized in the general life of society. In this the Christian faith agrees with Karl Marx's criticism of religion. The church reminds men of their human destiny, which surpasses the provisional character of what exists, and mediates to them participation in final salvation, in the midst of a present which is alienated from its own truth. The church can only credibly remind society of its temporary nature, and can at the same time only preserve access for men to the future of God through communion with Jesus, if it is mindful of its own temporary nature.

The criteria of the church's apostolic mission, its unity and its catholicity (or universality) also have their essential foundation in the future salvation of the rule of God, which has already been made available to us in Jesus Christ. For the missionary charge to the apostles, which was the foundation for the church's continuing apostolic mission, rests on the fact that the future salvation of the whole of mankind has already appeared in the history of Jesus and especially in his resurrection from the dead. That is why the church's mission is directed towards all men; and that is why universality is one of its own criteria. Yet the church, in being truly catholic, is never already perfected, but is always still on the road to full realization of its universal destiny. None the less its form at any given time can be the expression of this destiny and thus itself be already catholic. This destiny will find its representation above all in the unity of Christians with one another. As long as Christendom remains divided, the church, in the plurality of churches, can only incompletely, and not without culpable distortion, represent the common destiny of mankind, in accordance with the unity of God and Christ, and with the unifying spirit of love. It is only when it is one and universal that the church can preserve its holiness, its bond with the one God and Lord of all men. It can, of course, also only find its way back to unity by reflection on its holiness: the differences in the Christian community can only lose their dividing significance when there is consciousness of the temporary nature of church order and forms of doctrine, over and against the future of the rule of God and of the one Lord Jesus Christ – also over and against the bond in the Spirit of divine love, with all the consequences that has for the self-understanding of the churches. It is only in this way that the path will be free for growing mutual respect and co-operation – which is the only realistic way to the emergence of a new unity without uniformity between Christians.

This mutual recognition is, of course, only possible without destroying the acknowledgment of the one divine truth if it embraces faithfulness to the Christian past, to the church of the martyrs. And it is only possible, too, if the multiplicity of forms of belief and ways of life can be understood and justified on the basis of the unity of truth itself, as being for the moment still differing forms of recognition and expression of the one hope and the one faith, in which Christians can know themselves to be united, beyond the differences in their understanding, in common participation in the holy, which is to say in the saving truth of the one God.

The Forgiveness of Sins

If the communion of saints is to be understood as being originally participation in the holy, then this formula must be deeply
related to the forgiveness of sins. For forgiveness of sins characterizes Christian participation in salvation. It is at least the most
immediate effect of the nearness of God mediated through Jesus
Christ and the attendant perfecting of mankind into wholeness,
or salvation, in the life of the believer. Forgiveness of sins has to
do with the present effect of the divine salvation appearing in
Jesus Christ on the life of the person who is united with him;
whereas the final words of the Apostles' Creed – the resurrection
of the body and life everlasting – describe the future, perfect
participation in salvation towards which the forgiveness of sins
points.

Participation in the holy, forgiveness of sins and the future
hope therefore belong together. The forgiveness of sins is here
the negative expression for faith's communion with God,
mediated through Jesus, which is paraphrased as participation
in the holy, and on which hope for the eternal life of the resurrection from the dead is founded. In the positive sense, the real
riches of salvation owned by Christians are participation through
the Spirit of love in the life of God revealed in Jesus Christ.
Forgiveness of sins means liberation from everything which
divides us from God and therefore from a fulfilled and free life.
But men are most deeply separated from God by the self-
centredness of their lives, which is sealed through life's forfeiture
to death. This is not surmounted by the way in which indivi-

duals join together in communities, for on the one hand these only replace individual egoism by group egoism; and on the other they are still characterized by opposition between the individuals and the group, which usually end in certain indivi⁄ duals exploiting the common interest for the sake of forcing through their special concerns, contrary to those of the others. That is why forms of human community among men remain entangled in the dialectic of individual self⁄centredness. This would only be surmounted in a community of people under the token of the truth of God, removed from all man's despotic choices, in which the contrast between individual and com⁄ munity would consequently be overcome. But the history of the Christian church shows clearly the barriers which are built up even here by the present conditions of human existence, through its self⁄centredness and forfeiture to death. Forfeiture to death goes together with self⁄centredness. That is why forgiveness of sins and hope for a new life in communion with God belong inalienably together. And both are mediated to believers through their bond with Jesus Christ.

That is the meaning of Christian baptism. For the ancient church, the forgiveness of sins was intimately connected with the act of baptism. Here the connection between the communion of saints and the forgiveness of sins has a quite definite institu⁄ tional reference. Baptism unites the baptized person with Christ, or more precisely with the death of Christ, so that the person who is baptized dies to his own sinful life, in hope of the new life of the resurrection of the dead which has already appeared in Christ (Rom. 6.3ff.). With the mention of the forgiveness of sins and the hope of the resurrection, the Apostles' Creed turns at the end to the meaning and the force of the baptismal event to which the baptismal candidate is drawing near when he repeats the baptismal confession of faith. The immediate occasion for the whole creed finds its expression here. This is still more evident in other early creeds, in which forgiveness of sins and baptism were expressly linked with one another. Thus many Greek baptismal creeds, like the Niceno-Constantinopolitan Creed of 381, talk about 'one baptism for the forgiveness of sins'. This stress on baptism as something taking place once and for all is a reminder of the early Christian view that the forgiveness of sins is also given to us once and for all. The exclusive link between liberation from the burden of sin and the act of baptism led to the abuse that baptism was often put off as far as possible to the end of a person's life, because this seemed to lessen the danger of an irreparable relapse into sin. But this interpretation of baptism also gave the baptismal act the earnestness and depth of a complete reversal of existence. The view which came to prevail from the third century onwards that a 'second repentance' was possible for the backsliding baptized was at first only applied in exceptional cases. But from the early Middle Ages onwards the custom of infant baptism and the influence of monastic investigation of conscience in popular instruction meant that the forgiveness of sins was detached from its connection with baptism, and that repeated repentance and forgiveness, in the framework of the institution of regular auricular confession, became normal practice in the Christian life. Even the Reformation and the pietism which has largely given its stamp to Protestant devotion down to the present day were still influenced by this mediaeval attitude towards repentance.

When the forgiveness of sins became separate from and independent of baptism, this contributed to an obscuring of the connection between forgiveness and the hope of the resurrection. Today it is hardly evident any more that sin and the forgiveness of sin are a matter of death and life. The act of baptism made this clear to the early church; for the baptismal candidate only gains forgiveness of sins, together with the hope of the new life which has appeared in Christ's resurrection, when – united with the cross of Christ – he dies to his own life. Yet the church was right in not confining forgiveness of sins to the unique act of baptism; for though dying with Christ can indeed be antici-pated symbolically in a particular act, it none the less continues through the whole path of our mortal life until the hour of death. Even so, for the Christian understanding of salvation it is of decisive importance that the forgiveness of sins as a subject of Christian devotionalism is not isolated from the resurrection hope guaranteed through communion with Christ. Detached from the latter, sin and the forgiveness of sins become the slogans of a piety moralistically narrowed by its continuing struggle against the Law.

This piety is narrow, because it makes experience of sin the central theme of life in general, and forgiveness an end in itself, instead of a passage to a new life, for which it liberates and gives courage. The meaning of the forgiveness of sins is simply not understandable and convincing on its own. In modern times a Christianity which takes its bearings from the problem of guilt has increasingly come up against lack of understanding and mistrust among people who do not feel themselves to be sinners and who consequently believe that they do not need the message of the forgiveness of sins either. The number of such people is growing today, since the present-day mind has ceased to accept traditional morality as being valid as a matter of course. Must these people first be convinced of the binding nature of a moral demand, so that they feel conscious of being sinners and in need of forgiveness in the face of a 'radically' exaggerated interpreta-tion of this moral demand? Such an interpretation of the Christian message seems narrow, forced and not very convincing. It does not touch the really fundamental problems which people find in life; instead it first creates artificial problems, so that it can then recommend their solution. That is why Nietzsche rated Chris-tian morality and the mood which revolves round sin and forgiveness as hostile to life. We can only realize the positive meaning which the Christian message of forgiveness has for life if we recognize its relation to life's fundamental problems, which lie deeper than the moral ones. Life's fundamental question, however, is presented by the inescapability of death, which threatens life with the feeling of meaninglessness in view of the subjection to death of all human achievements and ideas. It is only against the background of the fate of death that the depth of substance in the Christian talk about sin and guilt proves itself; for it shows that the subjection of our existence to death is the result of its self-centredness. In the measure in which we strive for the fulfilment of existence through the enrichment of our ego, everything ends when that existence ends, and the ego especially also remains empty and dissatisfied.

Sin means going astray, failing to find the source of life in our search for life. The going astray consists in every man's striving for the fulfilment of life through enrichment of his own ego, separated from others and from God. But if God is the author of life and is the living one *per se*, then separation from God is bound to lead to a failure to find the fulfilment of life which is man's desire. Its immediate result is to be seen in the forfeiture to death of all human existence. Thus sin appears as a fundamental structural element in the constitution of human existence. The point at issue is not primarily individual faults; it is rather the faulty foundation of our existence as a whole, which merely finds expression in this or that mistaken attitude or concrete fault. The moral approach isolates the concrete faults and judges them as being basically avoidable, because the nature of man is supposedly good. It is of subordinate importance here whether the avoidance of such faults is expected of the individual or whether the attempt is made to avoid them by an alteration of social conditions, from whose negative effects the individual is released. According to the Christian perspective these definitely wrong attitudes and faults are neither dramatized nor made light of; they are seen as the expression of a total human situation which has to be conquered, which is much too deeply anchored in the constitution of human nature for it to be capable of altera/ tion at its deepest level by an alteration of the social structure.

If sin as separation from God is directly demonstrated in the forfeiture of human existence to death, then the concept of the forgiveness of sins takes on a new meaning. For then the forgive/ ness of sins means the warrant to hope beyond death for a life in communion with God. This liberating hope will then, of course, also have its effects on our present life. So far the ethical aspect holds good. Alteration in the behaviour of men and in their common life is not a matter of indifference. But the concerns of humanity are not generated by moral action – happily not, as if it could not exist if moral aims were not successful. On the contrary, moral action and moral consciousness always for their part already presuppose the humanity of man, which is the subject of the religious theme. The meaning and scope of Christian talk about sin and the forgiveness of sin originates in this dimension, not in the dimension of an abstract moralism. Consciousness of this can only be acquired once more if we are conscious of the connection of sin and the forgiveness of sins with the questions of life and death.

The origins of the Christian message of the forgiveness of sins lie within the framework of these questions. When Jesus told a man that his sins were forgiven, he was saying that this man would partake in the salvation of the coming rule of God, and thus in the new life of the resurrection of the dead as well. Jesus could promise this because he knew that trust in the future of God – the deliberate turning towards the coming of his kingdom – is all that God demands of men. Anyone who trusts in God's future can be assured of salvation. Nothing can separate him from the living God. Everything that has separated him from

God until then has now been overcome. Anyone who accepts the message of the imminent kingdom of God has, in so doing, already received forgiveness of his sins. Anyone who accepts Jesus as the proclaimer of the rule of God is free from the burden of a past which closes the future of life for him. The forgiveness of sins is, therefore, the consequence of trust in the future of the living God. It is the dawn of future salvation, the light which the saving future of God throws ahead of itself upon our present lives. It thus already opens up, now, the freedom of a new beginning and a new perception of the past, as well as of the situation of the present. The forgiveness of sins confers freedom for a complete affirmation of the present moment, of which only the man who can be certain of a fulfilled future is capable.

If freedom has first to be vouchsafed through the forgiveness of sins, that means that man is not free on his own account. The latter is not only presupposed where self-development through the free choice of the individual counts as a simple and immediately realizable way of achieving freedom; it is also assumed wherever man is given the task of self-liberation. Self-liberation through emancipation, i.e., through the casting off of all ties which limit freedom, is only a reasonable demand if man is already free in himself and is only prevented from exercising his liberty through inauspicious external circumstances. If man were in himself free in this way, then the full exploitation of all his predispositions and needs (as his right to the exercise of his own liberty) would in fact have to be demanded, as it is often demanded today; and the varying interests involved in self-development would have to be treated as having, basically speaking, equal rights. Experience teaches us, however, that not only do different people's needs for self-realization collide with one another; they also often only provide a substitute for the satisfaction expected and not infrequently cheat men of the chance to live truly fulfilled lives. If, however, the ways in which men look for self-realization so often go astray – for that is what the word sin means – then they are obviously not yet in possession of true freedom. True freedom must then first be conferred on them and revealed from outside, in contrast to their supposed momentary needs and to all that men already are in themselves.

This is the major question thrown up by the spiritual situation not only of the present day but of the whole of modern times: is man already free in himself, or must he first be freed, even *from* himself, in order to partake of true freedom? It is the latter which the Christian faith is acknowledging when it confesses the forgiveness of sins. It was already the heart of the doctrine of justification maintained by the sixteenth-century Reformers that man is not of himself free, but achieves true freedom through faith in the promises of God. For the Reformers, however, the substance of the liberating promise was the forgiveness of sins. Thus the Reformed doctrine of justification maintains that it is only through trust in the promise of the forgiveness of sins given in Christ that man achieves freedom – freedom which liberates man even from himself for his own true self, because it has its foundation outside ourselves (*extra nos*) in God and in his revelation through Jesus Christ. With this central thesis of its doctrine of justification through faith in God's promise, the Reformation stands in opposition to certain tendencies of modern self-understanding (tendencies which were active even then) according to which man is already free in himself. This does not mean, however, that it is opposed to the modern understanding of freedom in general. On the contrary, the assurance of God which is behind the doctrine of justification was the strongest impetus for the liberty of the individual against the power of socially sanctioned convictions. It therefore did pioneer work both in the history of political freedom and in the criticism of tradition, which in the period of the Enlightenment was directed against unsubstantiated claims to authority on the part of the Christian tradition and the warring churches especially. In the process the assurance of God inherent in the still traditionally bound faith in justification was replaced by a 'natural' knowledge of God, removed from the conflict of the churches, as the basis for the self-assurance of reason. Consequently assurance of God could ultimately appear as a mere human projection and the ground was cut away from the idea that freedom is founded in the divine reality fore-given to men, which has first of all to free men for freedom.

With this, however, the principle of freedom itself must ultimately appear as an arbitrary one, without any claim to absolute truth. Detached from its religious motivation in the freeing of man for freedom, freedom coincides with the caprice of individuals, with the freedom which man supposedly already has once the external restrictions on its use disappear. But the licence of untrained caprice is bound to bring the principle of freedom as a whole into miscredit. In contrast, freedom's justification on the basis of assurance in God's forgiveness of sins remains an indispensible leaven for the continuance of a free society, at least in our cultural sphere – a leaven which goes on working even through its secularized forms as long as its religious origin is alive.

Rightly understood, therefore, the preservation of true freedom, and with it the humanity of man, is committed to the Christian acknowledgment of the forgiveness of sins. This can only be so because freedom derived from faith does not lead a man astray *from* himself, but brings him *to* himself. It is true that acknowledgment of one's own sins also means a detachment from oneself. But that is only one side of its meaning. The acknowledgment of sin is always acknowledgment of oneself also, the expression of one's readiness to take over responsibility for oneself. Seen in this way, Christian consciousness of sin does not need to be the expression of a denial of the self and enmity towards life; on the contrary, it can be understood as an affirmation of life, even where life is distorted and travestied. The very acknowledgment of sin then appears as an act of freedom; for true freedom is responsible freedom: only in the taking over of responsibility for himself does a man become identical with himself. Consequently freedom is measured against the standard of readiness to know oneself as responsible both for oneself and for one's own sphere of life, with everything that happens or is neglected in it; for man is not himself as an isolated individual but as a member of his society and a part of mankind. He achieves identity with himself to the degree to which he does not seek the faults and failings of his sphere among other people but accepts the guilt and the responsibility himself. In this way he identifies himself with his sphere of life and takes the task of its reform on himself. Even in this sense acknowledgment of sin is not an expression of lack of freedom, which is only overcome by forgiveness. On the contrary, lack of freedom expresses itself in the suppression and denial of one's own guilt and co-responsibility. To look one's own guilt in the face, if it is not the expression of utter despair over oneself, is only possible through trust in forgiveness. In this way it already evinces the freedom towards oneself for which the forgiveness of sins liberates us.

The Resurrection of the Body, The Life Everlasting

Whereas the forgiveness of sins signifies the present saving effect of baptism and 'participation in the holy' in general, the resurrection of the body describes its future consummation. The people who are now baptized into the death of Christ and who in dying are bound to his cross, have through their communion with Christ the hope of partaking in the future in the new life of the resurrection of the dead, which has already appeared in him and which already gives those who are baptized power for a new life in faith and hope (Rom. 6.4ff.). The forgiveness of sins and life in faith, hope and love through the power of the Holy Spirit are the present dawn of future life in communion with God; and the Christian hope of the resurrection of the body is directed towards this consummation.

We already discussed the expectation of the resurrection of the dead earlier, in connection with the resurrection of Jesus. I do not want to repeat what I said there (pp. 97ff.) about the meaning of the Christian resurrection hope; about its general human relevance as the answer to the question of the wholeness of human existence, which finds no solution this side of death; and about its difference from the Greek belief in immortality. The contrast to the Greek way of thinking (which was only able to conceive of life beyond death as the continued life of the soul, separated from the body) is expressed by the particular stress of the creed's formulation when it talks about the resurrection of the *body*.

Some of the ancient Christian creeds which have been passed down to us heighten the statement still more and talk expressly about the resurrection of *this* – i.e., this present, mortal – body. That corresponded to the Pauline saying that '*this* perishable nature must put on the imperishable, and this mortal nature must put on immortality' (I. Cor. 15.53). The stress on the identity of the body in spite of its transformation is directed against the Platonic idea of the rebirth of the soul in a different body. It means that a man's identity depends on the uniqueness and non-recurrence of his physical existence. That is why the creed insists on the identity of the matter of 'the body' with a rigidity which must already have seemed barbarous to the Hellenistic world, even though people did not then know as we do that organic matter is renewed several times even during the lifetime of the individual.

But the stress on material identity does not need to exclude the idea of the immortality of the soul completely. On the contrary, Christian thinking has generally united the two actually heterogeneous ideas of the immortality of the soul and the resurrection of the body. The reason for this is that the resurrection of the dead was conceived exclusively as an event in the horizontal sequence of time. The resurrection of the dead was not expected to take place immediately after the death of the individual, however, but, according to Christian tradition, was to happen to all men simultaneously at the end of our present world and history. This suggested the question about the existence of the individual in the transitional period between the time of his death and the time of the future general resurrection of the dead. Here the idea of the immortality of the soul offered itself, to bridge the temporal gap between our present life and the future life of the resurrection of the dead. The continuity given by the continued existence of the soul seemed indispensable, in order to guarantee the personal identity of the future life with the present mortal one; even though the existence of the soul in separation from the body did not count as a full human exist-ence, since according to Christian thinking from its beginnings, the unity of body and soul was essential for full humanity. In view of the problem of the personal identity of a person between his death and the future general resurrection, and in view of the importance of personal identity for a man's personal responsibi-lity at the Last Judgment, it is understandable that since 1513 the Roman Catholic church has condemned the idea of the mortality of the soul as heretical, and has raised the immortality of the soul to a binding doctrine. In spite of this, it is doubtful whether a man's personal identity, and his responsibility at the judgment seat of God after death, is dependent on the assump-tion – so hard to reconcile with our present human knowledge – of a soul independent of the body, and hence surviving even the body's death. At all events, this assumption does not make the Apostles' Creed one whit more comprehensible when it states that not only the present body but its matter, the flesh, is to partake in the future resurrection. The identity of our present 'body' with the future resurrection reality remains inconceivable as long as one only adheres to the linear sequence of time. On the other hand, the theological concerns which are the substantial basis for the absorption into Christianity of the idea of the immortality of the soul can be better satisfied by a profounder view of the reality of time.

For the apocalyptic understanding of time held by early Christianity, that which is to be revealed on earth in the future already stands ready in divine concealment ('in heaven'). This was the logical progression which led from the identification of the risen Christ with the future Messiah and judge of the world to the conviction of his already present, though still concealed, universal rule at the right hand of God the Father. The same logic applies to the Christian resurrection hope: the future resurrection of the dead will reveal what already forms the secret of our life history for the eternal God who is present in our life. In the light of this unique intermingling of time and eternity, the strange words of the Gospel of John become understandable: he who believes in the Son already has eternal life. Thus the evangelist makes Christ say: 'He who hears my word and believes him who sent me, has eternal life; he does not come into judgment, but has passed from death to life' (John 5.24). The future of the final consummation is already present in a hidden way, and for that reason the final decision can already be made now, in the encounter with Jesus. That does not mean that according to John this decision is not a matter of the future. But as a decision in the future it is already present in a hidden way. That is why in the following sentence the Johannine Christ can let present and future flow paradoxically into one another: 'The hour *is coming*, and *now is*, when the dead *will hear* the voice of the Son of God, and those who hear *will live*' (5.25). In the Epistle to the Colossians (2.12) the baptized already enjoy present participation in the resurrection of Christ (which according to Paul is still an affair of the future; Rom. 6.5, 8). It is questionable, however, whether Colossians really diverges from Paul essentially here, since according to the Epistle to the Colossians the participation of Christians in the resurrection of the dead is only a now present reality in divine concealment: '. . . you have died and your life is hid with Christ in God. When Christ who is our life appears, then you also will appear with him in glory' (Col. 3.3f.). Here, too, we have once more the apocalyptic interlacing of historical future and hidden present in the eternity of God.

One could interpret this interpenetration of time and eternity in the sense that that which already exists in the eternity of God is independent in its reality of whether it will be revealed in the future or not. This would be to conceive eternity, and therefore God, too, as being timeless, and then whatever happens or does not happen in time would have no meaning for eternity, because everything that is still future in time would already have been decided in eternity. Such a view of eternity is not reconcilable with the Christian faith, for its consequence would be that either the course of the world (including everything that is evil or absurd) would be fixed by God in every detail from eternity; or the whole of human history, including the incarnation, would have no importance for God's eternity at all. But Christianity rests on the belief that this temporal history is, on the contrary, of decisive importance for God himself. Thus the interpenetration of time and eternity is rather to be grasped in the sense that the eternity of God is itself still dependent on the future of the world. The future revelation of the rule of God does not only reveal what is already decided even without this happening. It rather finally decides for the first time that from eternity God was the all-determining reality. In the light of the future of God it can therefore be said with John and the Epistle to the Colossians that in the hiddenness of God the believer now, already, has eternal life; that he now, already, partakes in the resurrection of Jesus. But this then means that the continuity of our present life with the future life of the resurrection of the dead must not be sought in the linear sequence of time, but that it lies in the hidden-ness of the eternal God, whose future is now already present for our lives. In this vertical dimension of our present life, the truth about this life – for judgment or salvation – is already present, the truth which has none the less still to be decided in the course of our life. Accordingly the future life can now conversely, really be understood as being materially identical with the present one; for the content of this future will be what fills the still-hidden vertical dimension of our present life – though of course in the way in which it appears in the light of the future of God which is and remains in a hidden way eternally present to all things. In this sense, then, the phrase about the resurrection of the body is in fact to be taken quite literally: it is really the same body, it is the whole extension of our present life, which will either perish at the judgment of God under its contrast to its human destiny or will be immortalized and glorified through participation in his immortality and glory.

This transformation of our mortal life, however, does not mean a frozen rigidity, as would be the case if eternity were to be viewed as timelessness. On the contrary, the Apostles' Creed supplements the hope of the resurrection of the dead, which was taken over from the credal forms of the Christian East, by a mention of the eternal life which awaits those raised from the dead. At this point the Niceno-Constantinopolitan Creed talks about the life of the world to come, thereby indicating the close connection of eternal life with the future of God. At the same time there is a suggestion of the difference in kind between eternal life and the life of the present. The life of the future world is not the resumption and endless prolongation of this life, along the same temporal line; it will unfold its dynamic through growth in the vertical dimension of our present life.

The transition of our present mortal life to the future world, i.e., the resurrection of the dead, was expected by the ancient church as an event which affects all men equally and which will come about at the end of all previous history and of the previous world. It was not thought of as being an event which happens to every single individual, perhaps immediately after his death. The salvation of the individual, the wholeness of his existence which had remained a fragment because of misfortune, error and death, is linked together with the destiny of mankind in the idea of a common resurrection of the dead at the end of the history of the present world. This also finds expression in the association of the general resurrection of the dead with the Last Judgment and with the full revelation of the kingdom of God, which will complete man's social destiny. For from its very beginnings the expectation of the resurrection had to do with the problem of the life of the individual, with the question of his participation in the fruits of salvation, which were promised to the chosen people and to mankind. The question about the confirmation of God's righteousness in the life of the individual person gave rise to the idea of a compensation in the next life for the negative balance of the present one. The fact that the resurrection of the dead and the judgment of the dead were none the less thought of as happening to all individuals together, at the end of our present history, and as being the beginning of the kingdom of heaven of the endtime, links the fulfilment of the human destiny of the individual with that of all other individuals and of human society.

In the secularization of Christian eschatology, which went on from the eighteenth century onwards, this link was lost. The goal of a perfect society in peace and righteousness – a classless society without the domination of man over man – was turned into a programme to be realized by man himself under the conditions of the present world. This modern faith in the future has, however, no longer any answer to the question of the share of individuals belonging to earlier generations in humanity's future realization in a perfect future society. This makes clear how doubtful is the readiness of modern revolutionary movements to sacrifice the happiness of the individual for the supposedly better future of mankind – as if mankind did not consist of individuals, and not merely people belonging to a future rulerless society at that. Mankind thought of in contrast to the sum of its individuals is only a horrible abstraction. The negation of the individual which is inherent in this abstraction shows its inhumanity in extremely concrete terms wherever such ideas are translated into political reality. The completion of the human destiny of mankind can only be thought of as the common fulfilment of the human destiny of all individuals belonging to mankind. And precisely this is the case in the classic Christian doctrine of the common resurrection of all the dead, which coincides with the dawn of the rule of God: without a general resurrection of the dead and a Last Judgment – that is to say without the participation of all individuals – there is no kingdom of God, and mankind is not perfected. This yardstick is appropriate and indispensable in controlling the misuse for political purposes of the idea of a perfected mankind. It is a control because it reveals the inhuman character of such proph-ecies, which are usually put forward in the name of humanity.

On the other hand impulses for the renewal of political and social life also constantly proceed from the idea of the future kingdom of God in peace and righteousness. For what hope in the rule of God is about is the fulfilment of man's social destiny. The presence of the coming rule of God in the mission of Jesus, and Christian faith in Jesus as the Messiah of God's coming kingdom can hence as little remain without social repercussions as can a self-understanding of the church orientated towards the future of the kingdom of God.

Yet it is not without significance that Jesus turned to the individual with his message of the nearness of the rule of God; he did not come forward as a social or political reformer. This characteristic is not merely a temporarily conditioned result of his expectation of the imminent end of the world. Jesus' re-jection of the title Messiah, with its political impress, contains the permanently significant indication that there is no direct approach to the kingdom of God via political change, but only, conversely, social effects deriving from religious trust in the kingdom's nearness and its power to determine the present. The link between the fulfilment of the kingdom of God and the general resurrection of the dead reminds us that all political renewals of society inspired by the eschatological hope are only capable of realizing a remote analogy to the peaceful order of the kingdom of God. The degree to which this really succeeds depends on the extent to which the social and political order enables its members to realize their individual destiny, which does not have to be identical with the satisfaction of all subjectively felt needs. A society's degree of humanity, however, is also measured against the candour of its relationship to the past of mankind in general and its own nation in particular. And individual life, too, is not only woven into present society but also into history, in which its depth lies. For the kingdom of God embraces the earlier generations of mankind as well as the coming ones, and hope for the coming of the rule of God does not only expect salvation for a last generation; it is directed towards the transfiguration of all epochs of human history through the fire of the divine judgment, which is one with the light of the glory of God.